PENGUIN BOOKS

FUNNY BUGGERS

Karl Chandler is a Melbourne comedian. He is in love with short jokes. He's extremely busy performing live stand-up, writing for TV, recording his popular podcast, 'The Little Dum Dum Club', pouring hours down the drain on Twitter, writing for TV, and accidentally repeating himself in his bio.

T0363598

FUNNY BUGGERS

THE BEST LINES FROM AUSTRALIAN STAND-UP COMEDY

EDITED BY KARL CHANDLER

PENGUIN BOOKS

UK I USA I Canada I Ireland I Australia
India I New Zealand I South Africa I China

Penguin Books is part of the Penguin Random House group of companies
whose addresses can be found at global.penguinrandomhouse.com.

First published by Penguin Group (Australia), 2011

Cover design by Alex Ross © Penguin Group (Australia)
Text design by Laura Thomas © Penguin Group (Australia)
Typeset in Adobe Caslon by Post Pre-press Group, Brisbane, Queensland
Printed and bound in Australia by Griffin Press, an accredited ISO AS/NZS 14001
Environmental Management Systems printer.

National Library of Australia
Cataloguing-in-Publication data:

Chandler, Karl (ed.)
Funny buggers : the best lines from Australian stand-up comedy / Karl Chandler (ed.)
9780143566250 (pbk.)
Australian wit and humor.
Popular culture — humour

828.402

penguin.com.au

CONTENTS

CONTENTS

FOREWORD

Thanks for buying this book. I say that because I can tell you're not someone browsing in a bookshop. Why would anyone pick up a book about jokes, and start reading the foreword? A fool, that's who. You're no fool. Are you? You're probably not. You've bought the book, and damn it, you're going to get your money's worth. Even if you have to plough through a dullish, unnecessary chapter-thingy to feel like you're getting value out of your purchase. Good for you, you shrewd (and bored) customer.

Honestly, I think the foreword is a bit of a weird part of a book. Particularly in this one. I mean, it's taken me a fair while to write, but if you skipped this section and went straight to one of, say, Tom Gleeson's jokes, that'd be fine by me. I guess it'd just be everyone else who'd discover the location of the hidden treasure that I'll reveal in the next few pages. I mean, where would you even keep all those dubloons? You're better off without them. Forget it.

This aim of *Funny Buggers* is to be a time capsule for this talented (as well as generous) generation of Australian stand-up comedians. All of the contributors to this book have provided some of their favourite lines, which have then been sorted into categories. And if there's a favourite comedian of yours who's missing from, it's probably because they were too busy to respond to my emails. Or, they hate me. So if there's a well-known comedian absent from these pages who doesn't seem to be that busy at the moment, you can figure out their feelings towards me.

There is a great new breed of comedians coming through in this country, evidenced by the strength of material here. Not only are there many famous TV and radio personalities littered throughout these pages, but those same pages also contain a lot of new talented names on the rise. If you're reading this book ten years after it was printed, some of those names may even be well known by now. Then again, some may also be using this book as bedding in a park somewhere. But, hey, I'm not their mum (in most cases). They can work out their own careers. I put them in this book; I can only do so much.

Funny Buggers aims to showcase the strength of Australian comedy at the moment. But then, humour has always been at the core of who we are. As a nation, we don't take ourselves too seriously. We're optimistic in the face of adversity. Maybe it's just too hot to think about it.

Having a laugh is as important to the typical Australian as sunshine, mateship and beer. Well . . . it's as important as sunshine and mateship, anyway. Some say our humour evolved from our origins as a convict colony. That being stuck in a barren, harsh new land, shackled in chains, led to our brand of self-deprecating humour. In a way, humour allows people to release the tension brought about by terrible experiences. This would also explain the anti-authoritarian, ironic and dry qualities our humour is known for. Plus all those classic manacle jokes we still know and love today.

These origins led to a fine humour culture being created. From the pantomime, burlesque, vaudeville, musical comedy and circus of the nineteenth century, through to radio plays, comedy revues and cabaret, into the boom time of stand-up comedy in the 1980s and our world-famous comedy festival in Melbourne, then on to all the hilarious sketch comedy, sitcoms, panel shows and public transport timetables that entertain us currently.

There's a great live-comedy scene in this country. Whether it's at big clubs or at little boutique comedy nights, there are hundreds desperate to get on stage, make people laugh and get as many free drinks as they can.

After you've been through this book, the talent of this current crop of comedians should be obvious. If you like their work, reward them. Go and see them at your local comedy club. Buy tickets to their show at the closest comedy festival. Send them a dirty message on Facebook. Do your bit.

I'd like to thank all of the lovely comedians who contributed to this book. Not only are they very funny, but they are all genuinely nice people to have helped form a great snapshot of Australian comedy.

Australians love to laugh. At ourselves, at others, whatever. And *Funny Buggers* proves that we love to make each other laugh, and we do it bloody well.

I hope you enjoy the book.

Karl Chandler

P.S. That treasure is in the ocean. To the left. No, I said LEFT.

ALCOHOL AND DRUGS

I have a drinking problem. For many years now I've been drinking solids.

CHARLES BARRINGTON

I tried to quit drinking but it's hard. You smokers, at least if you want to quit you've got the patch. What have we drinkers got? Nothing! I tried to make my own patches once. I just ended up covered in beer labels. I looked like a spare fridge in a bogan's shed.

JON BROOKS

Why is tequila the only drink that you never have alone? Tequila: party drink. Metho: lonely drink.

MICHAEL CHAMBERLIN

I saw some youngsters sitting out the front of Liquorland, and they asked me if I could buy them some beer. Why not? I thought. Then I found out they were just really lazy 23-year-olds.

SAM SIMMONS

I had three drinks in under half an hour on an international flight. When I ordered my fourth, the flight attendant said, 'Do you know that alcohol affects you twice as much at this elevation?' I said, 'That's fine. I don't plan on driving the thing.'

DAVE THORNTON

People say smoking makes exercising harder. That's ridiculous. Smoking makes exercise easier. Because it makes anything into exercise.

DANIEL TOWNES

I think non-drinkers are arrogant because they reckon they're good enough company sober.

MAT KENNEALLY

I know someone who was driving their car along recently and got pulled over because they were going too slow. Which worries me. Because that probably means you can get pulled over for driving too sober. 'I'm sorry, sir, you're going to have to come down to the station and have a few drinks. You're driving dangerously under the limit.'

ANGUS HODGE

Stubby holders have funny things written on them. I saw this stubby holder once that read, 'Beer is the answer. Does anybody remember the question?' I read that and thought, 'Yeah, I do. I think the question was "What legal drug ruins more families, helps people crash their cars, helps people fight friends, fight strangers, helps relationships end, and helps my dick stay soft? What fizzy fluid helped me urinate on my girlfriend once?" Beer is the answer.'

DAVID QUIRK

Everyone does drugs. How many sandwich bags do you think have actually been used for sandwiches?

SHAYNE HUNTER

I was on the website of a beer manufacturer and they were proudly bragging about the characteristics of their target consumer. They were like, 'This person is individualistic, they're a risk taker, and they're optimistic about the future . . . ' And I was like, 'That describes anyone after six beers.'

BEN DARSOW

I tried cocaine once, but I didn't inhale.

DAVE BLOUSTIEN

If you want to quit smoking, you need to replace the 'action'. I used to smoke rollies. So now I just carry around a miniature sushi-making kit.

MATT OKINE

Many alcoholics start as fine diners who realise red wine goes extremely well with red wine.

DAVE BLOUSTIEN

I found a message in a bottle. It said, 'Out of beer and envelopes.'

BRUCE GRIFFITHS

A lot of groups come out against binge drinking. It seems every day there's something in the media about it. So a friend and I decided to make it more interesting. Every time we see or hear the word 'binge' in the news, we do a shot.

ANGUS HODGE

To me, smoking is like disrespecting women or killing a midget. I don't do it, but it's still cool when James Bond does.

JACK DRUCE

My mum likes a drink. Preferably from a box.

JOEL CREASEY

In the early days of medicine, alcohol was used as an anaesthetic. What sort of build up is that for major surgery? 'Well, Mr. Jenkins, I'm afraid we're going to have to amputate your left leg. So skol, skol, skol!'

PAUL CALLEJA

My granddad was a belligerent smoker. At his request, when he died we had him cremated and his ashes blown into the face of a complete stranger.

GAVIN BASKERVILLE

There are picture warnings on cigarette packets now to scare smokers. Pictures of clogged-up lungs, black arteries, a gangrenous foot . . . A gangrenous foot? Who holds a cigarette between their toes?

DANIEL TOWNES

An epidural is evidence that no matter how good the drugs were that you took at your birthday party, on your actual birthday, your mum had better.

YIANNI AGISILAOU

You've got to want to quit smoking. Before I did, I spent years defending it to my friends. Especially the athletic ones who were always going on about it: 'Why don't you quit smoking and take up a sport? Get some exercise. You'll feel better about yourself.' What can you get from sport that you can't get out of smoking? It makes you out of breath. It makes you smell. And why do it recreationally? To keep skinny? So it's the same thing. And my friends would say, 'Smoking is not a sport. Smoking can kill you.' Well, then, smoking is an extreme sport.

DANIEL TOWNES

If LSD makes people hallucinate and see things, I think we should be giving it to blind people.

DAVO

I don't understand why alcohol is legal and pot isn't. I have never had a stoner try to glass me. Well, at least not that I'm aware of. He might have been trying to, but just couldn't muster the energy.

SHAYNE HUNTER

There's an ad that says, 'Ice. The drug that scares other drug users.' So I've started using it. For protection.

OLIVER PHOMMAVANH

I think you know your drug habit is out of control when you go to the pawn shop and it looks exactly like your living room used to.

GREG FLEET

I think drugs are bad. And that's why I think they should be legalised. So they can make better drugs. Like, one company might get the idea of putting fluoride in meth. That way, in the before and after pictures of users, as the faces are getting worse, the teeth are actually getting better.

SHAYNE HUNTER

I've never done ecstasy for the saddest reason of all – because I can't swallow tablets. And I think it is way too embarrassing to be at a nightclub and ask a dealer for a pill and a scoop of ice-cream.

NICK CODY

I don't know if this is a common drug experience, but I was on acid at a music festival in the bush and I needed to take a piss more than anything in the world. But at that moment, everything was too beautiful to piss on. It took me nearly an hour to realise that my piss was made of the same atoms as any thousand-year-old tree and everything was one thing, and then I ran around for the next hour pissing on everything and everyone I could.

ERIC HUTTON

There's this product I saw, it's a small white plastic tube that you suck on; it's filled with nicotine and is supposed to help you quit smoking cigarettes. Now, I don't need to quit, but I do want to start smoking and have been looking for a way to ease into it.

ALASDAIR TREMBLEY-BIRCHALL

Cocaine is like Tetris. Once you manage to make a line, it immediately disappears.

YIANNI AGISILAOU

I don't encourage young people to take drugs. Because that will increase demand.

TOM BALLARD

Life is just an experience. What is the highlight of most people's lives? When they look their newborn baby in the eyes? That feeling is just chemicals in your brain. It's only a matter of time before they make a drug that gives you the same feeling. Some woman could be in the toilet, doing 'Newborn' off the toilet seat . . .

SHAYNE HUNTER

ANIMALS

Dogs don't have first aid. Instead when they get sick they eat grass. That's a dog's answer for everything. 'Oh, I've got a sore paw . . . better eat some grass! Oh, I've got a sore tail . . . better eat some grass!' But it doesn't work, it just makes them vomit. Then they think, 'Oh, I keep vomiting . . . better eat some grass!'

MICHAEL CONNELL

My landlord doesn't allow pets. So if anyone asks, I have a live-in girlfriend named Mr Boots.

MANFRED YON

Someone asked me if I was a cat person or a dog person. I thought about it and realised I hate water but I love doing my business in my neighbour's sandpit. So I'd have to say I'm a cat person, literally.

JONATHAN SCHUSTER

I'm a beekeeper. Someone once gave me a bee and I kept it.

CHARLES BARRINGTON

I saw an ad on TV for a drive-through pet shop.
I thought, 'Drive-through pet shop? Who needs
a kitten *that* quick?'

MICHAEL CONNELL

They say cats always land on their feet. So I bought a
cat with no feet and threw it out the window. It landed
on another cat.

BRUCE GRIFFITHS

I believe the RSPCA was created by accident after
a horrible spelling mistake at an Aretha Franklin
concert.

ROB HUNTER

I was putting on my shoes, and I noticed there was
a spider web in one of them. That is one ambitious
spider.

TONY BESSELINK

I think Fido is telling me to kill my parents, but who's
the crazy one: me or the homicidal dog?

MANFRED YON

A pony has 0.5 horsepower.

KARL CHANDLER

Once I went snorkelling and saw the weirdest-looking school of fish. So strange that I actually laughed out loud. Then I felt bad because I realised it was a 'special school'.

MARK TRENWITH

My friend was telling me about a shark he saw. He said it was huge, and it had to be at least 15-foot long. But that just doesn't impress me. It's not because I'm not afraid of sharks. It's because I can never remember how long a foot is, and things just aren't as exciting when you have to measure them in Subway sandwiches.

LAURA DAVIS

Why are fish still getting caught? Haven't they figured it out yet? Hooks are bad! A 'school' of fish? What are they teaching down there?

PETE SHARKEY

I saw a squashed snail on the footpath. Proving that 100 per cent of snail deaths happen in their home.

JOSH EARL

Eagles are faux-hawks.

KARL CHANDLER

I'm like a snake. I'm more scared of you than you are of me.

DAVID QUIRK

If you put a chameleon in front of a mirror, does it look like a chameleon or the mirror?

BRUCE GRIFFITHS

A biologist's discovery of a giant lizard in the Philippines that has a double penis has apparently led to the phrase 'flat out like a lizard wanking'.

TERRI PSIAKIS

An old woman called me 'possum' the other day, and I thought, 'How does she know I've been in her roof?'

JONATHAN SCHUSTER

Maybe pandas aren't mating because all their potential partners look like their mum.

BEC HILL

A man was hospitalised after being attacked by a wombat. I believe he's in the Intensive Embarrassment Unit.

ADAM ROZENBACHS

If an elephant and a fish ever have a baby together, that baby will be amazing in every regard. Except its memory, which I imagine would just be average.

ROB HUNTER

Who was the first lion tamer to come up with the idea of bringing a chair into the cage? What was the process of elimination? Did they begin with a table lamp and move on from there? That's why lions don't work in offices. Too many bad memories.

TRAVIS NASH

Do you reckon lions that live in the jungle have statues of Italian people outside their caves?

ANTHONY MENCHETTI

I put a bird bath in my backyard today. I've already told two birds off for running and one for doing a bomb.

PAUL CALLEJA

I found out that I had rats in my house, eating my food, and I was horrified. Not for health reasons, but because I worried that it would affect my enjoyment of the film *Ratatouille*.

TOMMY DASSALO

I dislike funnel-webs, because they're just showing off, really. Funnel-webs are like, 'We have one of the world's deadliest poisons,' and I'm like, 'That's good. What is it you think you're catching, precisely? Dragons? No. It's flies, isn't it? You can kill a fly with a well-aimed moonbeam. Using the world's deadliest poison to kill a fly is like using a rocket launcher to kill a kitten.'

SAM BOWRING

The law of relativity in action: 30 minutes in a car with a wasp and a chronic farter is equivalent to five hours driving alone. Note: the wasp and the farter are separate entities. I have no problem with insect flatulence.

MATT ELSBURY

Giraffes have the same number of neck vertebrae as we do. We have seven neck vertebrae, giraffes have seven neck vertebrae. They're just better at it, I guess. They can only run up to 40 kilometres an hour, though, so it's totally okay to ride one through a school zone.

LAURA DAVIS

I saw a guy wearing sunglasses and walking a greyhound. I was like, 'Man, that is a blind dude in a hurry.'

KARL CHANDLER

To protect the people on the beaches of Adelaide from sharks, they have what's called the 'shark plane'. It's an airplane that swoops down, using a car alarm to let you know that there's a shark in the water. But if you're in Adelaide, and you get swooped by an airplane sounding a car alarm, you don't think there's a shark in the water, you think someone has stolen that plane. It would make more sense if the plane played the music from *Jaws*, and they could speed the music up or slow it down depending on how far away the shark is.

FABIEN CLARK

Orang-utans are amazing creatures. They actually build a nest for themselves in the trees and a roof for their nest. Essentially they build a tree house for themselves and their families. Pretty amazing. Still not as good as humans.

THE CLOUD GIRLS

THE ARTS

The worst review I ever received said, 'The Eskimo language has over 25 words to describe snow. The English language, on the other hand, has just five words to describe "shit". And that's "An evening with Charles Barrington".'

CHARLES BARRINGTON

I haven't been doing comedy for very long. When I started, I went to my uncle for advice, as he said he used to do comedy. I asked my uncle, 'Can you show me one of your comedy acts?' He started, and about four minutes into it I had to stop him. I said, 'How do you even call that a comedy act? That was horrible!' And he said, 'Comedy act? I thought you said "sodomy act".'

JONATHAN SCHUSTER

I'm in the bad books with a lot of the other comedians. They think I've been stealing their jokes. I prefer to think of myself as one of Australia's finest cover comics. Cracking your favourite gags from the '80s, '90s and today.

TOM SIEGERT

I went to see my brother's school play the other day. His school put on a production of *Pulp Fiction*. He played the gimp. It's a tough role. I just felt really sorry for the kid who had to play Marsellus Wallace.

JEFF HEWITT

I was so proud of my first paid gig of $20 that I framed it. Now it's next to the receipt for the $40 I spent on petrol to get me there.

STEELE SAUNDERS

Being a comedian, if I ever committed suicide, I would try to go out in a funny way. Like maybe I'd try to hang myself from an umbilical chord. Or bleed to death from paper cuts inflicted with my birth certificate.

NICK SUN

I'm a self-deprecating comedian, but I'm pretty shit at it. I do apologise.

JEFF HEWITT

You're not allowed to say 'good luck' in the theatre. You have to say 'break a leg'. Conversely, one must never say 'I love you' in the theatre either. You have to say 'I hope you break your neck and die'.

CHARLES BARRINGTON

I'd like to go to a 'Puppetry of the Penis' gig with a group of naked females, sit in the front row, then yell out, 'Bend it now, funny boys!'

ANTHONY MENCHETTI

I'm a nerd because I read a lot of books like *Lord of the Rings*. But people always assume I'm going to have useful knowledge. They're like, 'Hey, Michael, can you help me fix my computer?' I say, 'No, I can't. But I *could* fix your Hobbit . . .'

MICHAEL CONNELL

AUSTRALIA

My family are from the country, so we celebrate Australia
Day the traditional way. We shift a small part of our fence
onto our neighbour's property. And then we shoot them.

MAT KENNEALLY

I find political correctness offensive. People in
Canberra feel they have a gauge on forward-thinking
social etiquette. It's like taking relationship advice from
an autistic teenager.

JACQUES BARRETT

I love how in Sydney they keep their bogans in the
western suburbs. As far away from the beach as
possible. As if they're afraid they'll de-evolve into fish.

DANNY McGINLAY

I was down at Sydney Harbour and I saw an Aborigine
playing this didgeridoo-styled techno really loud.
Clearly it's now their turn to say 'sorry'. If you find that
offensive, is it because you're really anti-racism or really
pro-*Ministry of Sound*?

STEELE SAUNDERS

I love living in Melbourne. We've got so many cool bars. Especially those ones with no signs that like to play hide and seek with you down dark, spooky laneways. 'C'mon, Justin, if you want a $10 beer you've got to find me! Boozy, dance-filled fun could be yours down this stinky, bin-lined alley . . . or maybe a stabby death! Come on! Toadie from *Neighbours* is here!'

JUSTIN KENNEDY

I tried to celebrate Australia Day the traditional way this year. I stole some land and shot an Aborigine.

NICK SUN

I grew up in Lygon Street in Carlton. I thought *Underbelly* was a documentary.

SIMON PALOMARES

My sister wanted to go sightseeing. So I took her to the Eureka Towers Skydeck in Melbourne. I was a bit nervous, so the guy there said, 'Just imagine you're on the ground floor.' I said, 'Well, I'd be pissed off I'd paid $60 to look out the window. I probably wouldn't have bought a picture of myself doing it either. Maybe you should try imagining you're better at your job.'

JOHN CAMPBELL

Last night I had a dream that the Queen Victoria Market in Melbourne had shrunk. I woke up and thought, 'That's a little bazaar.'

JASON CHONG

I just flew in from Adelaide and boy, are my arms tired . . . from masturbating. Well, until Tiger introduces in-flight entertainment, I have to provide my own.

JON BROOKS

Every Australian town has a suburb where they cram in all their dickheads. Except Adelaide, where they crammed them all into Lleyton Hewitt.

DANNY McGINLAY

In Adelaide, there are more disgusting rat's tails than in the black plague.

KARL WOODBERRY

I went on a date recently with a girl in Adelaide, where I live. The following day something clicked for both of us, and we realised that we'd actually already met and been on a date when we were fourteen years old. I told this to my friends in Sydney and they were like, 'Oh my God, that's fate.' And I answered, 'No. That's Adelaide.'

BEN DARSOW

There's no street crime in Adelaide because there's no point. Firstly, nobody's got any cash. Secondly, if someone tries to mug you in Adelaide, you're like, 'Geoff?'

DAVE BLOUSTIEN

Cabs in Queensland are designed to freak out Victorians. It really freaked me out when I got a white cab driver. I got all excited. 'Oh my God! You've stolen a taxi!'

DANNY McGINLAY

If you're tired of London, you're tired of life. If you're tired of Perth, you're tired of death. Or just tired.

MANFRED YON

Walbundrie was a small town. It had one shop, one pub and one prostitute. Mum found it pretty tough working three jobs.

THE NELSON TWINS

I'm a Torres Strait Islander. Not many people pick it. To be honest, though, I didn't even know. It wasn't until I was filling out a form the other day and there was a question that said, 'Are you Aboriginal? Or Torres Strait Islander?' And I thought, 'Well, I'm not Aboriginal. Clearly leaves me with one other option.'

GERALDINE HICKEY

We could never have a 9/11-type terrorist attack in Australia. Mostly 'cause our emergency services number is 000. You can't make a date out of that!

MIKEY MILEOS

Generation Y is so self-involved. I was at an ANZAC Day march and I heard a kid say, 'I don't know what they're marching for. When my sim card broke, I lost all my mates too.'

KARL WOODBERRY

Every name has a meaning. For example, my middle name is René. In Latin, René means 'reborn'. And in Australia, it means 'bash me'.

MICHAEL CONNELL

Our suburb celebrated Australia Day with a riot. I caught up with guys I haven't seen since high school.

OLIVER PHOMMAVANH

The Cronulla race riots confused me. What can you even say as an Australian race rioter? 'Go home! You were here third! We were here second!'

YIANNI AGISILAOU

Ned Kelly wore a bucket on his head because he had
stitches that the vet did not want him to lick.

ROB HUNTER

I think multiculturalism in Australia is good. My
theory on why we sucked in the 2010 World Cup
was that there were too many fifth-generation white
Australians representing us. I say bring back the
European guys from the last World Cup. They got
us through to Round 16 and united our country.
It was like: 'Australia out of defence . . . Lazaridis
moves the ball forward . . . passes to Okon . . . Okon
hits Viduka . . . Viduka lays it off to Bresciano . . .
Bresciano crosses to Grella . . . Grella striking
forward leaves it for Vidmar . . . Vidmar smooth to
Skoko . . . Skoko over to Aloisi . . . Aloisi out in front
of Popovic . . . Popovic scores . . . Guus Hiddink
ecstatic . . . Goal for Australia!' And I just thought 'Go,
you skips!'

BEN DARSOW

I'm a big fan of the Order of Australia medal,
because I think it really rewards the good done in the
community. My favourite one was when Ian Kiernan
won it for creating 'Clean Up Australia Day'. On the
news it said that since he'd created it, the initiative had

taken off in more than 130 countries. Which is great, because if 130 countries want to clean up Australia, none of us have to.

ANGUS HODGE

How can the Australian government crack down on internet piracy? They say, 'You wouldn't steal a car.' Well, no. But you stole a country. And not only that, but you burned a copy of England to do it.

DAVE BLOUSTIEN

We're the most famous people to come from Walbundrie. We're a lot like Prince Harry and Prince William. Except we've got the same dad.

THE NELSON TWINS

The only people who loved the Southern Cross more than bogans were ancient sailors. But they needed it to navigate. Maybe that's why bogans are getting it tattooed on themselves. It's some sort of bogan GPS. I can just imagine them waking up after a big party, looking at the sky, then looking at their tattoo and saying, 'Well, I'm in the right hemisphere; that's a start. Now where did I leave the Torana?'

JON BROOKS

Space is so bogan. I just saw its Southern Cross tattoo.

KARL CHANDLER

I feel sorry for people who have Southern Cross tattoos, if they're not drunk racists and just very passionate astronomers.

JACK DRUCE

The Australian flag has the Union Jack in one corner and the Southern Cross in the other. It makes us look like England with a five-star review. New Zealand only got four, but I think they were demoted a star because they use the word 'jandles'.

DAVE THORNTON

Overly patriotic Australians always preach from the same gospel. 'Respect this flag! My grandfather died for this flag! Respect this flag!' Okay, I will. My only question being: 'Why are you wearing it as a cape?'

MICHAEL CHAMBERLIN

Why are the most fervent patriots the same kind of people who wear Australian-flag boxer shorts? So burning the flag is bad, but smearing your disgusting cheese and onion perineum all over the Union Jack isn't?

BEN ELLWOOD

Calling yourself the most powerful person in Australia is kind of like calling yourself the coolest 48-year-old at a Justin Bieber concert.

MICHAEL CHAMBERLIN

When you go to Canberra, all the locals keep telling you, 'Oh, it's a planned city . . . Canberra's a planned city.' What they mean is that it's 'intentionally boring'.

MICHAEL CONNELL

I spent the day in this really weird suburb called Special. I didn't mean to go there. I just got on the wrong bus.

GERARD McCULLOCH

I was doing a show in London, and an Englishman came up after the gig and said, 'That was very funny. But I have to say, I don't think it's right what you Australians did to the Aboriginals.' And I said, 'Wait, wasn't that YOU?'

GREG FLEET

THE BODY

I'm shaving all my hair off before I lose it. It's my way of saying, 'You can't fire me. I quit.'

DEAN EIZENBERG

I don't have any body hair. Whenever I'm down the beach, people say, 'Ugh, have you waxed?' I always say, 'Oh yeah . . . I've also had my chest sunken, and my skin whitened. It's part of my new "nerd" look. I've also had my biceps removed.'

MICHAEL CONNELL

It was my birthday recently, and I got some pretty sweet presents. The best gift of all came from my parents, who got me genetic male-pattern baldness. It sucks to be young and losing hair, especially as I still have acne on my face. My head has got some serious Benjamin Button shit going on.

TOMMY DASSALO

I don't like it when guys with a full head of hair take the piss out of me for being bald. That's like me walking around someone in a wheelchair and saying,

29

'Check out my legs!' Or taking a blind friend to the cinema and saying, 'Enjoy the soundtrack!'

TOM GLEESON

I don't understand bald people. Apparently hair is just dead cells that are being pushed out the top of our heads. So if bald people don't grow hair, does that mean their insides are full of death? The only other possible explanation is that bald people don't grow hair because their insides don't die. They are immortal, bald people who live forever. Which would be pretty cool. But I'd still rather have hair.

TONY BESSELINK

I found out recently that the number-one reason guys start losing their hair is because their bodies are producing more testosterone. Which means the truth of the matter is, I'm actually becoming more of a man. So now when I look at younger guys with their Lego-men hairlines, instead of feeling insecure, I just think, 'Grow some balls, pussies.'

BEN DARSOW

People say you've got to get in shape. I am in shape. It's just a round one at the moment.

DAVE O'NEIL

I grew a beard. Not to compensate for my baldness but because when I'm clean shaven, babies keep looking at me and freaking out. They think I'm a giant version of them.

JIMMY JAMES EATON

My mates tell me I have a receding hairline. I say, 'That's because you guys are looking at it from the front. From the back this thing is advancing.'

BEN DARSOW

You know you're bald when one day in the shower you loofah your head. You've clearly said to yourself, 'Hey, buddy, forget about your hair. Let's just make it shiny!'

JUSTIN KENNEDY

I'm not scared about losing a little hair. I'm just afraid that in a few years someone will say, 'I like what you've done with your hair,' and not mean in its plural sense.

DEAN EIZENBERG

I've got massive sideburns. Someone once told me I had nice chops. I told them if they liked my chops, they should see my sausage.

ADAM KEILY

Sometimes people call me 'the man with the burns',
because I have sideburns. And because of my severe
urinary tract infection.

OLIVER CLARK

I went to Weight Watchers. I lost about 350 dollars.

DAVE O'NEIL

I get a lot of crap about my moustache at work. One of
my colleagues said, 'Daniel, your moustache is terrible.
Mine's heaps better than yours.' I said, 'Maree, would
you piss off? We both know old ladies grow awesome
moustaches.'

DANIEL CONNELL

I just got myself a pair of contact lenses. I had no
idea how blind I really was. It wasn't until I rocked up
at work the other day wearing my new lenses that I
looked around and thought, 'My God. Can someone
please tell me how long I've been working at Kmart
for?' I swear to God I thought I was a dairy farmer.
I kept wondering why women were coming up to me
all the time saying things like, 'Excuse me, miss, do you
know where the maternity wear is?' I was like, 'Piss off,
lady. Cows don't wear dresses.'

GERALDINE HICKEY

When you underline things, they stand out more. Which is why people with excellent noses have moustaches.

ROB HUNTER

Everyone used to say I was the roughest kid at school. I thought this was because I was feared and respected. It was actually because my eczema made my skin look like sandpaper.

MARK TRENWITH

My hands constantly shake due to a condition called Benign Essential Tremor. The only thing it is 'essential' for is if you never want to win a game of Jenga.

NICK CODY

I've always been thick of thigh. I once scalped a girl playing leapfrog.

HANNAH GADSBY

My body is a temple. Except on weekends when I rent it out as a beer hall.

ADAM ROZENBACHS

I'll never forget when the postman cut his hand. That was a real red letter day.

GAVIN BASKERVILLE

Tattoos are great for preserving memories. Otherwise I would have totally forgotten about that anchor.

KARL CHANDLER

I've always wanted to touch a baby's bum just to see what all the fuss is about. I've heard they're really soft but I've never touched one. For years I've been lying to people by saying things like, 'Your face is as soft as a baby's bum.' But I don't know what that feeling is. So, now I say things like, 'Your face is as soft as that bit below my armpit but above the elbow.'

JONATHAN SCHUSTER

I've learned to be comfortable with my own body. At least that's what I'm telling those biology students I exposed myself to.

XAVIER MICHELIDES

My penis is a foot long. Three inches exposed, nine inches subterranean. I call it 'The Iceberg'.

YIANNI AGISILAOU

Are people who fall asleep on the train just really lazy sleepwalkers?

JIMMY JAMES EATON

A piercing on your willy is called a Prince Albert. Let's face it, you can't charge a hundred bucks and call it 'A-hole-on-the-tip-of-your-knob'.

SIMON PALOMARES

I asked the doctor about lap band surgery, if he could put a rubber band around my stomach.
He said, 'Sure, we could do that, or we could put a rubber band around the big packet of chips you eat every night.'

DAVE O'NEIL

I work out at Doherty's Gym, which is a world-class bodybuilders' gym in Melbourne. It is full of guys who are just muscle on muscle on muscle. That is why I work out there, because any weights that I can possibly lift are always available. 'Any of you guys using these 2kg dumbbells? Didn't think so. Cheers! Also, is there a Body Pump class around?'

NICK CODY

The male body is like a factory. The testicles, that's production. The penis, distribution. All the rest, that's just marketing.

YIANNI AGISILAOU

I have a classic hourglass figure . . . with only about ten minutes left.

HANNAH GADSBY

The other day I got my penis caught in my zipper. It was stuck for three long hours. This was most embarrassing. This was even more embarrassing considering I was camping at the time, and it was the zipper on my tent. I was not a happy camper.

TOM SIEGERT

CELEBRITIES

I really admire Tiger Woods. To reach number one in the world in two different pursuits is quite an achievement.

PAUL CALLEJA

Lady Gaga has released an autobiography called *Poker Face*. But you can't read it.

BEC HILL

I can't stand it when celebrities are used in ads. Because half the time these companies are laughing in your face with the people they choose to endorse their products. Like when Olivia Newton-John was made the face of Nintendo DS Brain Training memory games. Play a few more levels, Olivia. You might remember where you left that boyfriend.

JON BROOKS

Thank you to Donna Hay for teaching me that 'semifreddo' is a frozen dessert, not a partially aroused frog.

TERRI PSIAKIS

George Orwell wasn't so crash hot. His predictions about 1984 were rubbish, and he thought animals could talk.

MANFRED YON

I only just found out that Stephen Hawking is British. I thought he was American, because of his accent.

BEC HILL

Gwyneth Paltrow has penned a cookbook. I believe it's a comprehensive list of all the things she has never eaten in her life.

ADAM ROZENBACHS

All good things must come to an end. Which probably explains why Richard Wilkins' contract runs until the year infinity.

SEAN LYNCH

During one of his binges, Charlie Sheen had a plan to make a 'family of porn stars'. He wanted to rent a house in his street and have porn stars young and old and probably a dog that's appeared in porn, living as a family unit at all times. So from the lead actor in one of the worst sitcoms ever produced comes the premise for what would surely be the best sitcom ever.

ERIC HUTTON

Do you think when the Queen goes to nightclubs she just uses old coins as ID?

YIANNI AGISILAOU

I don't know why Ben Cousins got that 'Such is life' tattoo. They were the last words of Ned Kelly, but Ben's got nothing to do with bushranging. He would have been better off getting 'Why not? Yeah' tattooed on his belly. They were the last words of renowned American drug-taker Timothy Leary.

TERRI PSIAKIS

I didn't get that sense of satisfaction I really thought I would when I finally finished reading Jack Osbourne's autobiography.

LOU SANZ

'Matt Damon is on fire.' That's either a great review, or an amusing news article.

BEC HILL

I got an invitation to a function. It said, 'Dress code: Smart casual'. I went as Stephen Hawking in pyjamas.

BRUCE GRIFFITHS

CHILDHOOD

When I was a lot younger, for about a year, I felt like a man trapped inside a woman's body. Then I was born.

YIANNI AGISILAOU

Babies are so gullible. There's one born every minute.

GAVIN BASKERVILLE

Probably the worst advice my parents gave to me was back when I was about seven. My mother said, 'Tom, don't be smart.' So I didn't. And quite frankly, I've been a bit of a deadshit ever since.

TOM SIEGERT

The tooth fairy teaches children about life. More specifically it teaches children about accepting money for body parts.

DEAN EIZENBERG

Our dad didn't even want us, so we were raised by dingos. But we got kicked out of the litter because we ate one of their babies.

THE NELSON TWINS

I grew up on a farm for the first five years of my life. But sadly, like a lot of people, we lost our farm in a flood. I can still remember the trauma. Watching my father poring over the insurance policy on the kitchen table, only to discover that we were not insured against flood. Now, I don't know if you've ever tried setting fire to a wet farmhouse . . . in a flood . . . but you need rocket-fuel to get that sucker burning.

BRADFORD OAKES

My mum wouldn't let me play video games when I was a kid because she thought they'd make me into a violent criminal. This was back when the most extreme game was Tetris. I don't know what she thought they'd make me do. Join a gang . . . break into shops . . . and stack their boxes?

MICHAEL CONNELL

When I was a kid, it was a simpler time. It was back in the day when fat kids were picked on because they were the minority. Now they're the majority, they're picking on the skinny kids. 'Ha ha, you skinny boombah. Hey, look at him; he doesn't sweat when he eats. We'd bash you, if we could catch you.'

MICHAEL CHAMBERLIN

Apparently there is a childhood obesity epidemic.
Yet at the same time childhood anorexia is at the highest
rate it's ever been. Why can't the skinny kids just eat the
fat kids and we'll kill two birds with one stone?

TOMMY LITTLE

When I was a kid, I wanted to grow up and become an
astronaut. So far I'm 0 for 2.

MIKEY MILEOS

Forget the evils of drugs or sex, the only advice I'm
giving my child is, 'Don't tattoo your face!' Because
when you tattoo your face, not only have you crossed a
line, you've coloured it in.

JUSTIN KENNEDY

I went for a drive in my car and I was playing the Mr
Whippy music really loud. You should've seen the
disappointment on the kids' faces when they came
running out.

PAUL CALLEJA

When I was a kid, I was scared of the dark, but then I
grew some balls and was no longer scared. Because my
balls glow in the dark.

XAVIER MICHELIDES

Why do so many boy scouts get molested when their motto is 'Be prepared'?

DON TRAN

I don't think it's wrong for three-year-old girls to wear a miniskirt, but only 'cause all of their other clothes are mini too.

MIKEY MILEOS

FAMILY

My dad got remarried recently. Turns out I'm now half Asian. So, suddenly, I'm good at maths.

ANTHONY MENCHETTI

My 74-year-old Spanish father was watching my fourteen-year-old emo son painting his nails black, and eventually he turned to me and said, 'I can do that with a hammer.'

SIMON PALOMARES

When my dad does a speech at a birthday party or a wedding, he doesn't have a set routine, but he does finish with the same sentence every time: 'But I haven't finished yet.'

TROY KINNE

I loved playing Twister with the kid next door. Left foot green, right foot blue, left hand red, right hand yellow . . . He was a weird-looking bastard.

BRUCE GRIFFITHS

I think when my mum sends a text message, she thinks you get charged ten dollars per word. Yesterday my phone beeped and for a second I thought I had got a text from Tarzan. It said, 'WE NANNAS, DINNER. YOU COME. WANT.'

TROY KINNE

Mothers love handmade gifts. I got mine a gift voucher. Stuff her.

MANFRED YON

When I told my mum that I was a little bit lesbian, she told me she didn't want to hear about it. She asked me how I would feel if she told me that she was a murderer. Fair call. I would hope that it was just a phase.

HANNAH GADSBY

When we flew back from the US, my mum and I got upgraded to business class. They give out so much free champagne in there, Mum couldn't handle it, and she drank about four glasses while she was still stowing her bags. It's a sad day when you have to pay duty tax on your own mother to get her back into the country.

JOEL CREASEY

It's really weird being identical twins, and knowing
what the other is thinking. We once played a game of
Rock-Paper-Scissors that lasted three years.

THE NELSON TWINS

My mum gave me the name 'Michael René' because
she wanted me to be unique. I guess knitting my pants
wasn't enough.

MICHAEL CONNELL

I went over to my mum's house the other day. Because
I live there.

JACQUES BARRETT

My mum said that my seven-year-old nephew
constantly gets away with murder. I thought, that could
be handy. Because I really hate this guy at my work.

DANIEL CONNELL

We gave my mum a plasma television for Christmas.
She doesn't like it because there's no room for a doily
on top. She stuck it on with sticky tape, and every
night the newsreader looks like a Muslim bride.

SIMON PALOMARES

When I was young, my mum used to say the rudest thing you could do during dinner was to sit with your elbows on the table. The night I dipped my balls in the gravy, she said, 'Tom, I stand corrected.'

TOM SIEGERT

I'm thinking it might be time to put my parents into a home. I mean, sure, they both still work full time, but you can never be too careful.

TOMMY LITTLE

The interest rates at my bank are really high. It's called 'the bank of Mum and Dad'. It's a great bank, though, because what happens is every time I fail to make a repayment, my loan is reduced by 50 per cent.

MAT KENNEALLY

I gave my parents a new car. It melted in the rain. The best gifts are those you make yourself.

MANFRED YON

I had my kids late in life. I timed it so as they're just getting out of nappies, I'll be getting into them.

DAVE O'NEIL

I've child-proofed my house. Bars on the door, the windows: there's no way they're getting in.

DAVE BLOUSTIEN

Babies. They're like tiny milk vampires.

BEC HILL

With three young children in the house, it's getting harder to tell which one is crying: me or my wife.

MIKE KLIMCZAK

My identical twin brother gets really annoyed at me when we go to parties because of the way I introduce us. I always say, 'Hi, my name is Justin. And these are my spare parts.'

THE NELSON TWINS

Finding out you're going to have twins is an amazing feeling. It's like it's your birthday and you're sitting at home waiting for the postman to bring you a present. Then the postman knocks on the door, but instead of bringing you just *one* present, he tells you your life is over.

BEN POBJIE

My kids are the reason I wake up every morning.
Because they're screaming.

DAVE O'NEIL

I'm pretty pissed off with my identical twin brother at
the moment. Last week he forgot my birthday.

THE NELSON TWINS

The only thing standing between me and my
mother's sense of approval is a teaching degree and a
prescription for antidepressants.

KATE McLENNAN

My family can sometimes be a little hard work. I got to
a point last Christmas Day when my aunty asked me if
I could 'Put the internet onto a CD' for her, and I just
thought, 'I am done with this family.'

TOMMY LITTLE

I'll never forget the last thing my Nana said to me: 'Put
a pillow on my face. It's time.'

ADAM VINCENT

FOOD

I'm so impatient, I have two-minute noodles al dente.

MICHAEL WORKMAN

My friend gave me the recipe for humble pie. But
I must have made it wrong. Because it was freakin'
awesome!

KARL CHANDLER

A gourmet pizza is where you take a pizza and screw it
up by putting stuff on it that should never be on a pizza.

MIKEY MILEOS

People say there is no more horrible taste than defeat.
So I assume defeat tastes like soy milk.

ROB HUNTER

I became vegetarian because when you stop eating meat
you halve your chances of dying of heart failure. The flip
side of that is that if you nag people with statistics like
that, you double the chance of being beaten to death and
not having the protein to defend yourself.

JACK DRUCE

I was having dinner with a girlfriend of mine. I ordered
fish and when I offered her some, she said, 'Oh, no,
I don't eat fish because I'm a Pisces.' I said, 'Wow,
because I don't eat scorpions.' She said, 'Because you're
a Scorpio?' I said, 'No. They're poisonous.'

CELIA PACQUOLA

Kebabs and one-night stands are pretty much the same
to me. Both only occur when drunk, both are sloppy
and you get halfway through and think, 'I can't possibly
finish this.'

TOMMY LITTLE

Of all the cakes my mother used to bake when I was
young, my favourite would have to have been her
carrot cake. Reason being, she used real carrots. It's for
that exact same reason that her mud cake wasn't overly
popular.

TOM SIEGERT

Put anything in the fridge and it becomes a salad. Fruit
turns into fruit salad. Pasta turns into pasta salad. Dirt
turns into garden salad.

CHARLES BARRINGTON

I don't eat KFC. I'm not putting anything in my mouth that comes from a company whose mascot is an old man with a secret.

JUSTIN KENNEDY

I walked into McDonald's, and the girl behind the counter said, 'If you buy a Big Mac, one dollar of the proceeds goes to the Ronald McDonald House.' And I was like, 'Get lost. I'm not paying that clown's mortgage!'

MATT OKINE

I heard a chef describe the food he cooks as 'honest food'. It made me wonder what 'dishonest food' is. Perhaps it's where you order a steak and it comes out of the kitchen and starts yelling at everyone, 'Hey! I'm a chicken!'

ANNE EDMONDS

Why is bottled water such a competitive market? Does it really make a difference what brand you are drinking? You'd have to be a real weirdo to leave a shop because they didn't have a particular brand. 'What? No Evian? Well, I'm not drinking Pump. It's got no taste.'

DANIEL TOWNES

I reckon macaroons taste like a My Little Pony shat in my mouth.

SAM SIMMONS

'Spam' comes from the combination of the words 'spiced' and 'ham', while 'Vegemite' comes from the combination of the words 'vegetarian' and 'hermaphrodite'.

XAVIER MICHELIDES

'Rocket salad'. That's a name that's disappointed a million kids.

KARL CHANDLER

My local bakery has a sign that says, 'Rolls 80 cents each, 5 for $4!' The only thing you save is having to do maths.

MIKEY MILEOS

To the clown who created fruitcake: those were two separately delicious things and you ruined them both.

ROB HUNTER

I do enjoy being a vegetarian. As far as I'm concerned, tofu is just like chicken. Except instead of flavour, there's just pride. A warm smugness that really hits the spot.

JACK DRUCE

I don't get how horse is any different to any other meat. Baby sheep are cute and cuddly, but lamb is heavily promoted as Australia Day fare. How's that any different to throwing a horse-sausage on the Cup Day barbie? Surely you'd just call it 'the meat that stops a nation'?

TERRI PSIAKIS

I ate a terrible sandwich from a 7-Eleven called 'Christmas chicken'. It better not return on me at Easter.

JIMMY JAMES EATON

My wife has turned me into a vegetarian. But it's not like she's a magician. She didn't go 'Shazam! Now you're a vegetarian.' She just stopped buying meat. And I don't know where you get that stuff from.

DAVID TULK

My personal trainer asked me, 'What did you have for dinner last night?' He was pleased with my answer and congratulated me on my discipline. It was lucky he didn't ask what I had for a midnight snack.

TROY KINNE

When you're in the kitchen of a prison, don't drop the soup.

KARL CHANDLER

I hate when you're at a restaurant with friends and someone suggests sharing food. I'm not into it. I don't get why it's okay when we're at the restaurant for someone to suggest that we share food, but later on when we're back at someone's house having a beer and I suggest that we share girlfriends, suddenly I'm the weirdo!

TOMMY DASSALO

So apparently it's considered bad luck to steal the coins out of a wishing well. But hey, turns out bad luck tastes exactly like a Mars bar.

SAM BOWRING

They have flavoured water on the market. Flavoured water. How hard is it to make really, really weak cordial?

DANIEL TOWNES

HEALTH

The other day I got a big pile of money and I burned it. Sorry, I mean I joined a gym.

CELIA PACQUOLA

Going to the gym regularly supposedly adds three years to the end of your life. Isn't that just the three years you spent *in* the gym?

YIANNI AGISILAOU

Owning a treadmill is great. Before that, when I wanted to walk, I had to open my door and stuff.

MIKE KLIMCZAK

Bulimia makes me sick.

TOMMY LITTLE

My best friend's mother is a new-age spiritualist psychic who believes in some weird stuff. Like that a crystal mined from the ground by a small African child controls whether or not you're going to have a good day, that you can lose weight by only eating white foods and that if you get cancer it's because you pissed off an angel.

KATE McLENNAN

HISTORY

I remember where I was when I found out JFK had been shot. I was lying on my bed, reading about it twenty years later.

GERARD McCULLOCH

The hardest thing for pirates when naming their baby is guessing what colour beard it is going to have.

ROB HUNTER

I found out that Einstein was dyslexic. Makes me think he wasn't even that smart, he was just trying to write 'EMU' and got lucky.

JOSH EARL

Those rioters at Cronulla should have read their history books because the last time young Australians took on Middle Eastern men on a beach, it didn't work out so well. Nobody's making Cronulla biscuits over this one.

MICHAEL CHAMBERLIN

All history and human achievement will eventually become nothing more than pub trivia.

BEN ELLWOOD

I was watching a documentary on Hitler's girlfriend, Eva Braun. According to the documentary, she knew nothing about the Holocaust. Which is obviously not true, because if she was anything like my ex-girlfriend, she'd be like, 'What's with the gas bill?'

DAVID TULK

HOBBIES

My friend just got a boat. Who wants to go vomiting?

MIKEY MILEOS

I love the Nintendo Wii because it simulates reality
so closely that kids build up a sweat without realising
they are almost literally playing the sport. One day
when I have kids I'm going to give them a bat and a
ball, and when they say 'What's this?', I'm going to say,
'It's the latest Wii. Now go outside and check out the
graphics.'

BEN DARSOW

Bus napping is a fun pastime, but I'm getting addicted
to the rush of fear and adrenaline when I think I've
missed my stop.

CHRIS KNIGHT

The game Hangman teaches children that if you are
not good at spelling, people die.

ROB HUNTER

I'm a quite a big gambler. Not with casino games like roulette or blackjack, I'm more of a 'no condom' kind of guy.

NICK CODY

They say kids see over one thousand simulated deaths on television every year. Lightweights. I kill more than that in half an hour of Grand Theft Auto.

BEN ELLWOOD

Scrabble. It's all fun and games until someone loses an 'I'.

GAVIN BASKERVILLE

Everyone's complaining about video game and TV violence. You want violence, play chess. No one complains when an eight-year-old kid plots to eliminate a race of people by strategically killing their monarch and religious leader. You're aiming to wipe out the other race because they're a different colour!

DEAN EIZENBERG

I found half a ping-pong table. After four weeks' practice, I'm unbeatable at ping.

BRUCE GRIFFITHS

I remember when I told my mum for the first time,
'Mum, I think I'm going to try to be a comedian.' She
said, 'You stupid girl! You can't change colours!'

CELIA PACQUOLA

Why do we need casinos? Wouldn't it be easier to put
the pokies in Centrelink?

MAT KENNEALLY

Don't play Cluedo depressed. I ended up killing myself
in the conservatory with the candlestick.

DEAN EIZENBERG

I love those video games where you play simulated
versions of iconic battles from World War Two. God
bless the Anzacs; they fought and died face down
in the mud so I would have the freedom to smoke
bongs and recreate their exploits from the comfort of a
beanbag sofa.

BEN ELLWOOD

LANGUAGE

Imagine a world without hypotheticals. You can't.

MICHAEL WORKMAN

You say amputated, I say amputatoed.

MIKEY MILEOS

If I had to pick one word I could do without, it'd be 'superfluous'.

KARL CHANDLER

My name is Hannah. Hannah is a palindrome . . . a word that's the same forwards and backwards. My entire family have palindromic names. Mum, Dad, Nan, Pop. And my brother, Kayak.

HANNAH GADSBY

Why do billboards point out that it's a 'house AND land package'? I thought the two were mutually inclusive. If you've bought a house without land, that's a boat.

DAVE THORNTON

The letter 'O' deserves more recognition than it gets. Without the letter 'O' *Sesame Street*'s The Count would be an entirely different character.

ROB HUNTER

How embarrassing. I only just realised I've been saying 'faux pas' wrong.

JOSH EARL

I'm not a fan of jumping on bandwagons. These new-fangled cars, though . . . Come on, everybody's doing it!

MANFRED YON

When unpacking my new wardrobe, I realised I don't wear two-thirds of my clothes. Mostly because that would look stupid.

ROB HUNTER

My friend said he was going to take a quick slash. He explained that was Melbourne slang for urinating. The next day I saw in the paper some guy was slashed to death outside a nightclub. That doesn't say a lot about the response time of police. He must have been there for hours, slowly drowning as his attacker made repeated trips to the 7-Eleven for Powerade.

JOHN CAMPBELL

Someone should tell Yoplait there is no French word for 'yum'. They're only embarrassing themselves. And me, when I say 'Mmmm, Yoplait!'

ALISON BICE

For years I thought that in France, Lego was just called 'Go'.

BEC HILL

So we need more words, I think, because the ones we have are far too imprecise. For example, we have no word for the feeling you get when you have seen one too many sitcoms do a send-up of Tom Cruise in *Risky Business*.

BEN POBJIE

The word 'dumb' has a silent 'b'. 'Deaf' should have a silent 'd'. And 'blind' an invisible one.

DEAN EIZENBERG

My favourite thing in the whole wide world, more than anything else, the thing I would choose in preference to the exclusion of all other things, is brevity.

YIANNI AGISILAOU

The first person who ever referred to his bicycle as a 'pushbike' was quite clearly using it incorrectly.

ROB HUNTER

'Osmosis' is a word I know, but I don't know how.

KARL CHANDLER

Ironically, the word 'chillax' makes me very tense.

STEELE SAUNDERS

I love reverse racism almost as much as I love Asians.

TOMMY LITTLE

Benjamin Franklin once said, 'Anyone who sacrifices a little freedom for a little security deserves neither and will lose both.' That's why I don't wear a seatbelt. I think that's what he was talking about.

MIKEY MILEOS

If there's one thing I can't stand, it's a guy with no legs.

BRUCE GRIFFITHS

The real menace to our society is reverse racism: the practice of backing your car over black people.

BEN POBJIE

I was at a funeral for my friend's grandpa, who was 96 years old. This lady got up and said, 'Well, the unthinkable has happened. Morris has passed on.' What is unthinkable about a 96-year-old man dying? When I see a 96-year-old, death is the first thing I think of. That sentence should have gone like this: 'Well, the unthinkable has happened. Morris has passed on. And then one week later he rose from the dead and violently raped a Galapagos tortoise.'

TOMMY DASSALO

I'm worried about leaving my inner child alone with my dodgy inner uncle.

KARL CHANDLER

I would never, ever write a joke in the form of a multiple-choice question because a) person who thinks that will b) funny should c) a psychiatrist.

FRANK WOODLEY

A traffic cone is an example of both a safety device and a way to pass the time at an intersection.

DAVE THORNTON

When someone calls you too easily offended, it's very
difficult to know how to react.

ALASDAIR TREMLEY-BIRCHALL

I got in trouble for writing 'I LOVE JEW'S' from a
grammar Nazi.

KARL CHANDLER

I met a ninja at a party one night. I went up to him
and said, 'Yo, wassup, my ninja?' Turns out, they don't
like being called that by white people. Just other ninjas.
Sorry, I mean, 'Asian assassins'.

JUSTIN KENNEDY

Letters can be numbers if you're into algebra. Numbers
can be letters if you're an idiot who has a personalised
number plate.

DAVE THORNTON

What do I think of wind turbines? I'm as big a fan as
they are.

YIANNI AGISILAOU

I don't understand the way rappers talk. What do they say 'word' for? 'Word.' Like they are explaining what it is they are actually saying . . . 'Word.' I go, 'Yeah, well, this is a sentence, motherfucker!'

DANIEL TOWNES

A good example of what the word 'subtle' means is its middle letter.

KARL CHANDLER

Only sblack people can say 'snigger'.

MATT OKINE

I think the reason radio ads have to be more annoying than any other kind of commercial is that no one's really paying that much attention to the radio. The real-life equivalent of a radio ad would be if you were sitting at work, trying to do something and a guy runs in and starts shrieking in your ear and rubbing semen in your eyeballs, and when you turn to him to express your frustration, he yells 'Commonwealth Bank' and then runs off and jumps out the window.

ERIC HUTTON

LITERATURE

I like to go to the library, get all the books on feng shui, then put them back in the wrong section.

KARL CHANDLER

I used to work in a bookshop. When I would ask people if they would like a bag for their purchases, I was always surprised when a person would say, 'No. Save the trees.' I would think, 'You just bought a book! There is one tree left in the paddock. Take it. It's lonely.'

HANNAH GADSBY

I'm tired of people blaming magazines for every single problem in their life. Aren't we giving these magazines a little more credit than they deserve? If you really need *Zoo Weekly* to tell you how to meet women, maybe female interaction isn't for you. If you really need *Cosmo* to tell you how to give yourself an orgasm, maybe owning a vagina isn't your thing.

MICHAEL CHAMBERLIN

I read this book called *The Game*. It's all about pick-up techniques and the laws of attraction between guys and girls. One of the techniques it talks about is that if someone is interested in you, what they might do is ignore you. So I'm feeling pretty cocky at the moment, because I went out last Saturday night and not a single girl came up to me.

BEN DARSOW

Some people have dream dictionaries. I have a dream thesaurus. So I don't know what my dreams mean, but I do know what other dreams they're like.

KARL CHANDLER

I like reading graphic novels. There a bookstore near my house that sells them, but the graphic novel section is right beneath the 'Queer Literature' section. So I worry that when I'm looking for the latest edition of *Iron Man*, some stranger is going to see me and think that I'm looking for a very different kind of iron man. Then I worry that because I'm worrying about it, that that automatically makes me a homophobe. I have a friend who's gay so I asked him about it. He said, 'It's fine, you're not homophobic. Sometimes I'm at that bookstore looking for queer literature and I worry that people are going to think that I'm looking at comic books and that I'm twelve years old.'

TOMMY DASSALO

I stopped writing a diary when I read Anne Frank's effort. That genre has been conquered.

HANNAH GADSBY

My mum gave me a copy of the *Karma Sutra*. Which, ironically, put me in an uncomfortable position.

KARL CHANDLER

MEDICINE

Why aren't smokers constantly being treated for smoke inhalation?

BRUCE GRIFFITHS

I'm a bit disappointed that in this day and age there are still people having scalpels left in them after surgery. Leaving a scalpel inside someone is like locking your keys in your car. The doctor's sewing up the patient, saying, 'Well, that was a successful operation . . . Shit! I left the scalpel in there! Nurse, pass me the scalpel so we can get him open and remove the scalpel . . . Oh. Wait. Nurse, grab me a coathanger.'

TONY BESSELINK

I'm a coeliac. That means I can't have gluten and gluten is in everything. It's in McDonald's, Hungry Jack's, Pizza Hut, KFC, all the major food groups. What I'm trying to say is: I'M FUCKING HUNGRY.

MICHAEL CHAMBERLIN

Acupuncture can cure anything. Except pins and needles.

GAVIN BASKERVILLE

On a form I was filling in, it had the question, 'Do you have any mental health problems?' I couldn't decide what to put down, so in the end I couldn't resist making a little joke. Because I wrote, 'Yes. I have split personalities. But I don't.'

CELIA PACQUOLA

I'm colour blind. I could be racist . . . I have no idea.

RHYS NICHOLSON

How did I become a coeliac? All I will say is never have unprotected sex with a loaf of bread.

MICHAEL CHAMBERLIN

Psychology starts with a 'p'. That's cruel. People who need psychological help are already in trouble, now you're just making it harder because they can't find it in the *Yellow Pages*.

DAVE THORNTON

I have an eating disorder. I have never skipped a meal in my life, but I live in constant fear of it happening.

HANNAH GADSBY

The pill is a labour-saving device.

KARL CHANDLER

I walked into a shop the other day because they were offering free hearing tests. The guy behind the counter said, 'Hi, how's it going?' I said, 'Good thanks.' He said, 'Congratulations, you passed.'

ADAM KEILY

I was in a pharmacy where the slogan said it was a 'good old-fashioned chemist'. Which is lucky because that was really my biggest problem with the pharmaceutical industry: far too modern. With all their precious science. I want Viagra just like Momma used to make.

JACK DRUCE

If the stick turns blue, it means you're pregnant. If it turns yellow, it means you're low in iron. If it turns grey, it means don't trust Virgos. Brown calls for extensive Senate reform. Black means 'Arrr, these are pirate seas'. Red means the father may be the young Mickey Rooney. And if it turns orange, it says that you're not pregnant yet but the way you're putting blokes away, it's just a matter of time.

MICHAEL CHAMBERLIN

MEN

As a man grows older, hair grows in places you don't
want it to grow. It grows out of your ears. Down your
back. And on your wife's chin.

DAVE THORNTON

I reckon that sometimes true love just comes down to a
matter of practicality. I decided that 'the bloke' was the
one for me when I got out of the shower one night and
saw that he'd put my pyjamas over the heater, so they'd
be nice and warm for me. At least I think that's why
he did it. Either that or he was hoping they'd catch
fire and I'd have to sit on the couch to watch *Star Wars*
with him in the nude.

TERRI PSIAKIS

I ran into a family friend who'd had a sex change
operation. She kept telling me how she used to be a
man. I told her, 'Technically you're still a man. To be
an actual woman, you'd need to remove your Adam's
apple, have a womb put in, and somehow genetically
remove the Y chromosome from each strand of your
DNA. In actual fact, the way that you think you can

become a woman by simply swapping a penis for some boobs, is inherently a massively male way of thinking.'

JOHN CAMPBELL

A guy once said to me that I'm only a lesbian because no man would sleep with me. Because men are notoriously the fussy ones?

HANNAH GADSBY

I was out to dinner with a friend who suddenly announced that all men think with their penises. I said, 'I know what you mean, mine did the sudoku the other day. All us men have been in the situation where you're stuck, unable to solve the nine-letter word in *The Age* only to hear a little voice cry out, "I think you'll find it's HYPERBOLE."'

SIMON GODFREY

I learned that according to research, older men are the worst offenders at not cleaning their hands after using the toilet. So remember that next time Grandpa offers to feed you grapes. I know I will.

SAM BOWRING

The best way to get men to turn up to something is to call it 'Ladies Day'.

YIANNI AGISILAOU

I moved in with my older brother and I don't think you realise until you move out of home for the first time how little you actually own. I owned nothing: no couches, no appliances, no cutlery, nothing. If someone came over, I would have to say, 'Just take a seat on the floorboards and I'll get you a handful of water from the tap.'

TOMMY LITTLE

The shortest man in the world already has a complex about his height yet they still rub it in his face by taking that photo of him next to the world's tallest man.

PAUL CALLEJA

Probably the only thing worse than having a weird flatmate who masturbates in the shower is not being able to say anything because he doesn't know you always watch him.

TOM SIEGERT

MONEY

I recently bought a house. Actually, that's not true.
I just wanted to say those words.

ADAM VINCENT

I was at the casino playing a machine and won five
hundred dollars. Then I realised it was an ATM.

DAVE O'NEIL

I'd like to be rich. Not even *rich*-rich. Just rich enough
to not care what colour the plates are on a sushi train.

MATT OKINE

I was rubbish at money laundering. I left the 10s in
with the 20s and they came out as 15s.

YIANNI AGISILAOU

MOVIES

I asked the guy at the video store to recommend a good mystery film. He suggested *Dude, Where's My Car?*

LOU SANZ

My favourite prank is to walk into a video shop, place an old Beta video-cassette copy of *Ghostbusters* on the counter, take out my wallet and say, 'I think there might be a fine on that . . . '

MICHAEL CHAMBERLIN

Why do they need that line 'Only at the Movies' at the end of every movie ad? Were there really that many people rocking up at Carpet Court demanding to watch *Schindler's List*?

JOHN CAMPBELL

I know people who said they didn't like the last Indiana Jones movie because it was just a bit over the top. What are you talking about? Did you see *Raiders of the Lost Ark* and think, 'Fuck me, what an amazing documentary?'

JUSTIN HAMILTON

I recently completed my novelisation of the *Lord of the Rings* film trilogy. Only to find out that I was pipped to the post by some other author: Mr JRR Tolkien. His version was very shabby. Numerous scenes in his book weren't even in the film!

CHARLES BARRINGTON

People tell me, 'You should read *Lord of the Rings* before you watch it.' I didn't have enough time so I bought a bootleg copy of the DVD with the subtitles on it. So I've now seen it AND read it. In English, Thai and Chinese.

DAVE THORNTON

I hate how *Twilight* changes the vampire mythology. We all know that if a vampire is exposed to sunlight, they burst into flames, right? Not in *Twilight*. They 'sparkle like diamonds'. Come on! What happens if you stake them through the heart? A kitten comes out?

DANNY McGINLAY

I don't understand this new-wave of incredibly good-looking vampires. How can they get their hair and makeup looking *that* good when they can't even see themselves in the mirror?

MARK TRENWITH

There's a scene in the movie *Chopper* where Chopper
Read is in prison and he gets stabbed by his friend.
But it doesn't play out the way a regular stabbing plays
out. Chopper acts as if getting stabbed doesn't bother
him, and it's the guy cutting him who is crying. And
I thought, at that moment, Chopper Read was very
much like an onion.

ALASDAIR TREMLEY-BIRCHALL

It strikes me that the cow that was lowered into the
pit of robotic dinosaurs in the film *Jurassic Park* would
not have known that it was in a movie. They always
say 'No animals were harmed' in the credits afterwards.
I think they should say 'No animals were harmed in
the making of this movie. However a number of them
were *seriously* confused.'

LAURA DAVIS

Every time I open a cupboard or a wardrobe, I give it a
tap on the back wall, just to see if it might be a portal
to Narnia. This isn't from a sense of magic or childlike
wonder, it's just that I have a lot of cool clothes and I
don't want any fauns stealing them. I'm talking to you,
Tumnus.

CHRIS KNIGHT

If there is one thing I've learned from *Back to the Future*, it is that if you avoid sleeping with your mum in the past, and force your dad to fight the school bully, you are more than likely going to score yourself a sweet four-wheel drive!

TRAVIS NASH

Snow White lived with seven dwarves and everyone was cool with that. I know if I met somebody who lived with seven dwarves, I'd have quite a few questions, most of which would be sexual; the rest of which would be sexual. With just a tiny few about shelving.

MICHAEL CHAMBERLIN

The formula for a good biopic is, 'the shitter the life, the better the film'. I'm sure Anne Frank was a good writer for a kid, but I don't think anyone would have read her diary if she was just a reasonably good volleyball player or worked in a florist's or something.

ERIC HUTTON

I felt bad for Luke Skywalker when Yoda told him that his crush, Princess Leia, was his sister. That's an intergalactic cock block.

STEELE SAUNDERS

Opening scene of *The Da Vinci Code*: the curator of the Louvre gets shot by an albino monk. He doesn't call the cops, he writes an anagrammed message in his own blood that only two people on Earth can understand. Why? I understand he might not have a mobile phone, but he could at least write 'An albino monk just shot me! Shit!' Except obviously it's in French: '*Un albino moine juste abattu moi! Merde!*'

DANNY McGINLAY

I think it's wrong that a movie with the title *Speed* is about a bus driver and not a truck driver.

KARL CHANDLER

I'm the type of guy who refuses to see the movie *Apollo 13*, because I think 'Bugger it. I haven't seen the first twelve, I won't really know what's going on.'

JUSTIN HAMILTON

I saw the movie *Super Size Me* recently. Man, there's a lot of product placement in that film.

ALASDAIR TREMLEY-BIRCHALL

I went and saw a movie in 3D. It was a play.

KARL CHANDLER

I bought a DVD that boasted 'lots of added extras', but when I watched it, all it had were more people in the background.

GAVIN BASKERVILLE

I want to invent 2D glasses. Then when I walk down the street, it will feel like I'm watching a movie.

TOMMY LITTLE

I like the *Harry Potter* movies, but I prefer the series of video games that they're based on.

TOMMY DASSALO

Film and TV merchandising has become ridiculous. I saw a *101 Dalmatians* colouring book. How do you colour in a dalmatian?

MARK TRENWITH

I ordered the *Inception* meal at Barnacle Bill's. It's a bream within a bream within a bream. And curly fries!

CHRIS KNIGHT

MUSIC

Playing harmonica is really hard. With one hand, you have to hold the harmonica; with the other hand, you have to stop people beating you up.

MICHAEL CONNELL

Every time I see a one-man band perform, I am not surprised he has no friends.

ROB HUNTER

The other day I saw a three-year-old kid singing a Black Eyed Peas song. Finally, the lyrics seemed plausible.

JIMMY JAMES EATON

I think with most artists the last CD they make is their best. Their greatest hits.

MANFRED YON

The other day I saw a poster for the Kings of Leon tour. Their tour poster from three years ago was sooooo much better.

TOMMY DASSALO

I have a friend who's an Elvis impersonator. Well, I assume he is. He doesn't sing, he just eats a lot and wears a tracksuit.

KARL CHANDLER

How did Kurt Cobain die? See, sometimes suicide IS the answer!

MIKEY MILEOS

When I was younger, I was in a rock band called 'Shy Bladder'. Sadly, we couldn't play in front of each other.

JUSTIN KENNEDY

I read an article that referred to U2 as a 'supergroup'. Did I miss something? Is U2 a new supergroup made up of ex-members of U2?

TOMMY DASSALO

Endings of songs fall into two categories. Cold endings: where the songs just stops; and faded endings where the song just gets quieter and quieter. I hate those, it's weak songwriting. You wouldn't get that in any other medium. You would never read a book where suddenly there's less and less words on each page.

DANNY McGINLAY

We ran out of tiles when renovating my bathroom floor, so we just used Bon Jovi albums instead. Except you've got to be really careful because it gets slippery when wet.

MARK TRENWITH

Whenever I tell people I play the harmonica, they instantly get patronising: 'Oh, you play the harmonica! That's great! And you've dressed yourself! Well done!'

MICHAEL CONNELL

I was gutted when Radiohead cancelled their second Melbourne concert in 2004. Not only did I have tickets to the gig, but I'd won a competition to meet Thom Yorke backstage by sending in four barcodes from my brand of antidepressants.

THE BEDROOM PHILOSOPHER

Lady Gaga is really popular among gay people. She's our new god. To put it simply, Lady Gaga is to the gays what Nickelback is to bogans.

JOEL CREASEY

Australian music legend Michael Hutchence died masturbating with a belt around his neck. I think there's a lesson we can all learn from his death. Always wear pants that fit.

DAVO

If dance music makes you dance, and blues music makes you blue, then what does roots music make you wanna do? Oh, that's right: kill yourself.

DAVE THORNTON

We, like, changed our band name. We're called 'Rage Against The Sewing Machine'. We're all about anger and fashion.

THE BEDROOM PHILOSOPHER (from 'Northcote (So Hungover)')

The best musical collaboration I ever heard was between Nickelback and a power failure.

DAVE THORNTON

I like to imagine that when I'm skipping through songs on my iPod, all the musicians I have on my playlist are inside my phone waiting to see what I pick. And when I finally settle on one, the band high fives each other, and gives the finger to all the other bands and yells, 'Suck it, losers!'

HARLEY BREEN

I'm a big fan of all the old-school blues guys. I like how they all had cool 'blues names' like Willie 'Blind Boy' Fuller, or Curtis 'No Toes' Jackson. I want to have a cool name like that, but there's nothing that wrong with me. My blues name would be something like Michael 'Slightly Asthmatic' Connell.

MICHAEL CONNELL

OCCASIONS AND HOLIDAYS

On Halloween, I'm going to give out hash cookies. It's trick AND treat. But not in that order.

ADAM ROZENBACHS

It's amazing that Santa Claus got to the age he is without ever having worked out that he doesn't exist.

GAVIN BASKERVILLE

We should have a Valentine's Day but with health instead of love. Something like 'I-Don't-Have-A-Terminal-Disease Day', where we can all go around celebrating how lucky we are. There'd be people in wheelchairs complaining, 'I hate I-Don't-Have-A-Terminal-Disease Day. It's become too commercialised, it's just corporations selling you stuff you don't need.' And you'd be like, 'That's what dying people *always* say about I-Don't-Have-A-Terminal-Disease Day. They can never just be happy for anyone else.'

TONY BESSELINK

If I hadn't been so good at extinguishing birthday candles in one breath, I would have so many girlfriends right now.

CHRIS KNIGHT

I think I did pretty well with my Christmas shopping this year. I got my new baby niece a shirt that says 'My First Christmas' and I got my 89-year-old great grandmother a shirt that says 'My Last Christmas'. It's economical because if she doesn't die in the next year I can just re-gift it because she's so senile, she has no idea where she is.

RHYS NICHOLSON

For Christmas, my parents gave me a relaxation disc. The only CD player I have is in my car, so I keep falling asleep at the wheel.

BRUCE GRIFFITHS

In my day, for Christmas we got a memory stick. It was just a stick, and if you forgot something, Father would hit you with it.

THE BEDROOM PHILOSOPHER (from 'In My Day')

I hate Christmas lights. It makes it hard for me to tell which ones are brothels.

OLIVER PHOMMAVANH

I wish that during the minute's silence on Anzac Day, all kebabs would stop rotating as a mark of respect for soldiers of both sides.

ADAM ROZENBACHS

It seems like people start complaining about Christmas decorations being in stores too early earlier every year.

STEELE SAUNDERS

I stayed in the Hilton Hotel once. The room had everything, but at one point I rang reception. I said, 'Hi, this is David in room 224. There seems to be a problem with my microwave.' The receptionist said, 'There's no microwave in your room, sir.' I said, 'Yes there is. It's in the closet.' She said, 'That's an electronic safe, sir.' I said, 'Oh. Can you send someone up to get my pie out, please?'

DAVID TULK

PEOPLE

I'm not a spontaneous person. If I'm going to do something spontaneous, I have to have to give myself 48 hours' notice.

MICHAEL CHAMBERLIN

To people who win awards and say they are humbled: you are confusing yourself with one of the losers.

ROB HUNTER

I'm not a very organised person. In 2009 I spent more time trying to get the last olive out of a jar than I did planning my future. And I hate olives. They taste funny and hold me back from my dreams.

ADAM VINCENT

Inside every fat cannibal, there is just a skinny person trying to get out.

CHARLES BARRINGTON

Emos are goths who don't get enough pocket money.

SIMON PALOMARES

I went to a friend's place and they said, 'Make yourself at home.' So I asked them to leave. I don't want them taking my stuff.

DEAN EIZENBERG

I was on a tram, and sitting across from me were two elderly people. They didn't know each other. This was their whole conversation: the woman pointed towards the man's feet and said, 'Oh, you've only got one shoe on.' The man replied, 'Yeah, I've only got one leg.' If you don't find that funny, I cannot help you.

DAVID QUIRK

I've realised recently that I'm just an average person. You know, I'm not a great person, but I'm definitely not a horrible one either. Like, I won't park in disabled spaces but I will crap in their toilets.

TOMMY LITTLE

Do you ever go walking at night and look into people's windows? I do. My attitude with that is, as long as I've got momentum, I'm not a pervert.

ADAM VINCENT

Beggars are just buskers who don't like to show off.

GAVIN BASKERVILLE

The other day I saw someone had written 'Gays Are Evil' on a wall. But then on top of that, someone else had written 'Dinosaurs Are Rad'. How can you not feel good about the world when you see something like that? What that says to me is that no matter how much one person might 'hate gays', there'll always be someone else out there who likes pterodactyls way more. It's like that old game: paper covers rock, rock crushes scissors, triceratops eats homophobe.

TOMMY DASSALO

If the sun explodes, people with solar power are going to be super-annoyed. Because like the rest of us, they will be dead.

ROB HUNTER

There's no positive paranoia. You never think you're overhearing someone say something really nice about you. You never think you're hearing, 'See that guy over there? I really want to give him a trophy.'

ALASDAIR TREMBLEY-BIRCHALL

I believe there are benefits to being a pessimist. Because when you're a pessimist, you're never disappointed, only pleasantly surprised.

MICHAEL CHAMBERLIN

Everyone I know thinks that people are idiots. I think that's cynical. I think most people are smart and it's just that dumb people stand out more. It only takes one guy licking a window on a bus to make the whole bus look retarded.

SHAYNE HUNTER

I start every day by saying, 'I'm going to seize this day like it's my last.' I end every day by saying, 'I shouldn't have eaten that.'

TROY KINNE

I have to get new friends. Last year my friends threw me a staying away party. Next year they're planning a surprise funeral.

DEAN EIZENBERG

Sometimes I become paranoid about people wearing camouflage pants. You can't fool me. I know you've got legs.

JOHN ROBERTSON

Homophobia has got to be one of the least tolerated phobias in the whole phobia family. If somebody came up to you and said, 'I'm claustrophobic', you wouldn't say, 'Oh, you narrow-minded bigot! You discriminatory freak! You obviously haven't spent enough time in dark, narrow spaces. What about the cupboard? Mr Mop and Mr Broom are happy in the cupboard, but no! That's not good enough for you, is it, claustrophobe?'

LAWRENCE MOONEY

I saw a charity worker with a bucket that read, 'Please help blind people'. So I ran down the street, poking people in the eyes.

BRUCE GRIFFITHS

You don't see many condom machines in toilets anymore. They've been replaced with machines for tissues. Guess there's a lot more wankers now.

OLIVER PHOMMAVANH

I used to have a schedule with stuff on it like 'wake up'. Which is good because when I get up it feels like I've done something.

DAVO

You know when you kill a prostitute and you run away,
and you get that half-terrified, half-thrilled feeling?
What's up with that?

GREG FLEET

The other night before bed, I had to set an alarm for
11:30 a.m. the next day. It is very hard to look yourself
in the mirror and convince yourself that you're kicking
goals in life when you need electronic assistance to
not sleep through midday. The worst part is, I slept
through the alarm. I woke up and was like, 'Oh, well,
at least I'm awake in time for the end credits of *Ready,
Steady, Cook*.'

TOMMY DASSALO

I saw a hipster so trendy, even his moustache had a
moustache.

SEAN LYNCH

There are some things you can't shout. For instance
'THIS CAMOMILE TEA IS SOOTHING!' Or
'I JUST PUT THIS BABY TO SLEEP!' Or 'I'M
HIDING IN A LIBRARY!'

XAVIER MICHELIDES

I once spent a month with a blue bucket on my head. Because when you die, your life is supposed to flash before your eyes. And I think it would be kind of cool to go, 'Hey, check that out. I had a blue bucket on my head.' It diverts the attention away from not having achieved all that much in life.

ADAM VINCENT

POLITICS

Barack Obama's election meant a lot to me. My mother is an American, which makes me a US citizen. On top of that, when I was born, my parents were living off the coast of Africa. I know I may look like a skinny white guy, but that makes me an African-American. For me, Obama's victory was a victory for my people.

MAT KENNEALLY

The 2010 hung election was frustrating. It was like Australia sat down to do a shit and nothing came out. And now that we've got a result, I don't like the smell.

TOM GLEESON

John McCain ran for president at 71 years of age. If was elected, he would have been the kind of president you could assassinate with a common cold.

MAT KENNEALLY

Remember, disguised within every full beard is a Hitler moustache.

ALASDAIR TREMBLEY-BIRCHALL

I saw a woman blowing ciggie smoke in a small child's face, who was saying, 'I'm voting Greens, because when the oxygen runs out, I want to know at least I tried.'

LOU SANZ

The Labor Party said we needed a 100-million-dollar internet filter to stop people accessing child pornography. Internet experts said most experienced computer users could bypass the filter in a few moments. That means our government planned to spend 100 million dollars to mildly inconvenience paedophiles. That's like trying to stop bank robberies by dropping banana peels outside banks.

MAT KENNEALLY

I saw a sign that read, 'END ROADWORK'. I thought, 'I don't have that kind of power. You need to talk to someone from the council.'

BRUCE GRIFFITHS

I like to think that terrorists have a sense of humour. I want to believe that somewhere, sometime a suicide bomber's last words were, 'Pull my finger.'

GAVIN BASKERVILLE

My new dentist is excruciatingly thorough. Each time I'm sitting in the chair being prodded with a tiny sharp hook, I can't help but wonder why George W Bush tortured detainees at Guantanamo Bay? He could have got just as much information from them, and stayed within the bounds of the law, by insisting all detainees maintain perfect dental hygiene.

MAT KENNEALLY

Everyone hates the boat people. Everyone thinks they are coming here to steal our jobs. I'm not sure if you've been to a café or a restaurant recently, but do you know who's stealing our jobs? Backpackers. It's not the boat people, it's the plane people we should worry about.

RHYS NICHOLSON

The Climate Sceptics is a party that intrigues me. Is it a bunch of dudes who don't believe there's a climate? 'It's sunny outside.' 'PROVE IT!'

TOMMY DASSALO

Climate change sceptics are so optimistic. They're always reservoir half-full kinda people.

DANNY McGINLAY

PRODUCTS

I bought myself a shopping trolley the other day.
They're only a dollar each.

DAVE O'NEIL

Scented toilet paper is an example of a battle that
cannot possibly be won.

ROB HUNTER

I believe there's nothing wrong with going into a shop
and just buying toilet paper. But it doesn't feel all that
right either.

MICHAEL CHAMBERLIN

People who fold toilet paper instead of scrunching are
technically just making shitty origami.

TOMMY LITTLE

Toilet bowls must look at hand basins and think,
'You've got it easy, don't you?'

DAVE THORNTON

I bought a bathroom air-freshener in a fragrance called 'Mountain Air'. Because sometimes when I'm in the shower I like to pretend I'm at a higher altitude. It just makes the whole experience that little bit more extreme.

LAURA DAVIS

I was looking after my neighbour's daughter and she would not stop screaming and crying. So I got some of that Johnson's No More Tears shampoo and I just rubbed it in her eyes. She did not stop crying. It must have been out of date.

RHYS NICHOLSON

My girlfriend bought me a Seiko Sports 200, a watch that is waterproof to 200 metres. And I thought, thank God for that. Because I used to have a Seiko Sports 100 and that was so inconvenient. You'd be out in the ocean, diving down around 120 or 130 metres. Your head would cave in, your lungs would explode, and the doctor would say, 'So, what time did this happen?', and I'd be like, 'I dunno. My watch broke.'

LEHMO

I want to write 'Buy new pen' on my to-do list, but I can't.

KARL CHANDLER

My highlighter leaked. Now everything in my bag seems important.

KARL CHANDLER

They knocked back my application to own an automatic weapon. In response to the question 'Reason you need the gun?' I wrote: 'I want to shoot things.' What other reason is there?

BRUCE GRIFFITHS

I have Post-it Notes. But no one ever posts them. They're just sticky notes. Has anyone tried to post one? I have never received one in the mail. Maybe someone did send me one, but it stuck to someone else's mail.

DEAN EIZENBERG

I went into a magic shop, and asked a guy behind the desk if I could buy a bike. He said, 'Oh, sorry, we don't sell bikes. We're a magic shop.' I said, 'Exactly. Now make it happen.'

PETE SHARKEY

I took my wetsuit to the dry cleaners. He didn't know what to do with it.

GAVIN BASKERVILLE

RELATIONSHIPS

I'm in a long-distance relationship at the moment and I don't mind telling people that. Because it sounds better than 'restraining order'.

CELIA PACQUOLA

'You'll find someone when you least expect it.' This Friday night I'm going to stay at home, watch *Star Trek*, and masturbate.

OLIVER PHOMMAVANH

I went speed dating once, and I was a bit nervous. So I decided to go into it with a prison mentality. I got there and immediately stabbed the biggest girl in the room, just so the rest of them would respect me.

TOMMY LITTLE

My great-aunt said to me the other day that I shouldn't worry about being single because when she was my age everyone thought she was left on the shelf as well. Cold comfort from a woman in her 60s who's still single and wears sanitary napkins on her knees to do the gardening.

KATE McLENNAN

I'm tired of going to weddings where I know the couple isn't going to make it. Why should I spend a $150 on towels just because you didn't want to have 'the conversation'?

MICHAEL CHAMBERLIN

Couples that wear stripes together should be buried alive together.

LOU SANZ

I got dumped by a homeless girl. How dare she? Beggars can't be choosers.

OLIVER PHOMMAVANH

An ex-boyfriend said to me once, 'Babe, if I can't get steak at home, I'll go screw a cow somewhere else.' I only date vegetarians now. And lesbians.

KATE McLENNAN

I'm in my first long-term relationship. It's been nearly five years. Have you ever realised that you get the same options in a relationship as you do in a bushfire? Because you can leave early, or stay and defend.

DAVID QUIRK

Now that I'm engaged people ask me if I'm worried that 50 per cent of marriages end in divorce. To be honest, I'm more worried about the 50 per cent that end in death.

GAVIN BASKERVILLE

I went speed dating recently. I thought, 'There's two things I'm shit at. Let's make an evening of it.'

HANNAH GADSBY

I want to be with the woman of my dreams. The fact that she's a lesbian makes it difficult.

DEAN EIZENBERG

My friends say, 'Don't worry; there's plenty of fish in the sea.' Have you seen the sea lately? It's fucking polluted.

OLIVER PHOMMAVANH

My girlfriend took me on a romantic night out at the opera recently. During the show she reached over, grabbed my hand, and whispered in my ear, 'You know, we're never going to have this night ever again.' And I said, 'Look, is that a promise? Because this is the most boring day of my life.'

RAY BADRAN

I'm even getting turned down in my sexual fantasies.
I didn't know that could even happen. She gave me the
whole 'let's see other fictional people' talk.

DEAN EIZENBERG

My younger sister had a boyfriend who cheated on her.
Apparently he's a bit of a tough guy, but that didn't
stop me sending him a stern warning. I posted him a
bullet with a note attached, saying, 'Watch yourself,
or the next one will be coming a lot faster, pal.' He
sent me a text saying that I was weak and I was
bluffing. So I had no choice but to prove I wasn't
bluffing. I sent him another bullet, express post.

TROY KINNE

My ex-girlfriend left me because I wasn't supposed to
mention how big her vagina was. But somehow I just
kept putting my foot in it.

GAVIN BASKERVILLE

My ex has a new girlfriend, but I'm not really ready for a
new man. I know this because I have a hair growing out
of my nipple and every day I look down at it and think,
'When I'm ready for a man, I'll do something about that.'
It's not attractive, but does save cash on dental floss.

KATE McLENNAN

My girlfriend broke up with me because apparently
I'm too much of a 'tiger' when it comes to love making.
That's ridiculous. A tiger is the biggest compliment
you can get. To be precise, she said 'cheetah', but tiger's
the same thing . . . they're both jungle cats.

TROY KINNE

I love one-night stands. My favourite part about them
was that occasionally, on a Sunday morning, I would get
to take a magical adventure through a suburb I've never
been in. I say 'magical adventure', some of you might
say 'walk of shame'. Depends how you were raised.

NICK CODY

My girlfriend wanted to know if we were going to
be together forever. So she used the most scientific
method out there – the love calculator. Typed in our
names, worked out a percentage. Found out we were
95 per cent compatible. If my name was Michael.

OLIVER PHOMMAVANH

RELIGION

I believe God brought Jesus back from the dead as an example of how important it is to recycle.

ROB HUNTER

I gave up lent.

KARL CHANDLER

The priest at the church I used to go to declared everything the work of the Devil. You actually began to admire the work ethic of the Devil.

MICHAEL CHAMBERLIN

I'm not spiritual or religious; I believe in the here and the now. That, and betting on horses with the same names as family members is a sure thing.

KATE McLENNAN

If Noah had a wooden ark and saved two of each animal, he took a big risk inviting termites on board.

ALISON BICE

I think born-agains should take the metaphor of being born again even further, and not talk for two or three years.

HANNAH GADSBY

The Pope has finally said that condom use may be justified on occasion. He must be getting sick of his priests leaving all that evidence behind.

TOMMY LITTLE

The Pope is meant to be the best of the best. He's worked all the way up the ladder. He starts out as a brother, a father, an uncle, a monsignor, a bishop, black belt, leader of the opposition and then when he pulls the sword from the stone, he becomes Pope.

MICHAEL CHAMBERLIN

The Catholic Church lifted its ban on condoms. Sounds like a certain Pope Benedict XVI got someone pregnant.

ADAM ROZENBACHS

In the beginning, there was nothing. Then there was God . . . or, if you're an atheist, an even bigger nothing.

JOHN ROBERTSON

Of course, the true meaning of Easter is Jesus rising from the dead. One of my little cousins asked me how all that relates to chocolate rabbits, so I told her a story about how Jesus died on the cross, got buried in a cave and was then helped out by Frank, the giant bunny who told Jesus what to do. Then I realised that wasn't from the Bible, that was from *Donnie Darko*.

TERRI PSIAKIS

According to the Bible, Israel is 'the land of milk and honey'. That sounds like a great place to go to, if you have a sore throat.

MIKEY MILEOS

I always thought Jesus was still alive, but that's probably because I had a Choose Your Own Adventure Bible.

ADAM ROZENBACHS

I just happen to be an atheist; that's just my opinion. If you're religious, I'm not saying you're an idiot . . . but I am thinking that.

TOM BALLARD

I bought myself a figurine of Jesus. It's pretty special because on his face there's an apparition of a piece of toast.

JASON PESTELL

I'm losing faith in atheism. I mean, how am I supposed to believe in nothing if I can't see it?

KARL CHANDLER

I have a religious friend. I treat him better than all my other friends just in case he's right.

TOMMY LITTLE

Before Jesus became mainstream, he only had a cult following.

DON TRAN

I'm an agnostic suicide bomber. I'm willing to die for what I may or may not believe in.

JEFF HEWITT

There is now an 'atheist news podcast'. What could the news be? 'This just in . . . God is more not real than ever.'

STEELE SAUNDERS

Men are having ribs removed so that they can go down on themselves. It's ironic that God removed Adam's rib to create woman, and now men are getting another one removed so that they don't need her.

YIANNI AGISILAOU

SAYINGS

Throw your hands in the air like you just don't care.
Unless you're at an auction.

DAVE THORNTON

It's all fun and games until someone loses an eye.
Except in Operation, then it's just play on.

JOHN CAMPBELL

They say there's no rest for the wicked, but I reckon
they're just wicked due to lack of sleep.

MIKEY MILEOS

See a penny, pick it up. Curse 45 years of decimalisation.

GERALDINE QUINN

I don't know what kind of argument would get solved
by burying the hatchet. Unless it was an argument
about whether you can grow a hatchet tree.

SAM BOWRING

Don't throw all your eggs at one bastard.

KARL CHANDLER

If cleanliness is next to Godliness, you have a shit dictionary.

ROB HUNTER

You can lead a horse to water, but they're very hard to drown.

SAM SIMMONS

There used to be such honour among thieves. They even gave out high-achievement awards. Well, they didn't 'give' them out.

MANFRED YON

Some people say it's bad luck when a black cat crosses your path. This may be true, but as I discovered, if you happen to be mowing your lawn at the time, it could also be bad luck for the cat. They say cats have nine lives. Unfortunately, though, my mower has ten blades.

TOM SIEGERT

A bird in the hand means you probably just robbed a pet store.

GERALDINE QUINN

Two negatives equal a positive. Like the inheritance I got from my dead grandparents.

KARL CHANDLER

If you can't say anything nice about someone, they're probably a prick.

GAVIN BASKERVILLE

If your ears are burning, someone is talking about you. Or you are using your toaster incorrectly.

ROB HUNTER

Deciding to sit in a sauna is 1 per cent inspiration, 99 per cent perspiration.

KARL CHANDLER

If life hands you lemons, make lemonade. If a waiter hands you a lemon, just squeeze a little on your food. No need to be a jerk.

CHRIS KNIGHT

A lot of conflict in the old west could have been avoided if cowboy architects had just built their towns big enough for everyone.

ROB HUNTER

She sells sea shells by the sea shore. What an idiot!
They're lying on the beach for free.

SAM SIMMONS

There's no 'i' in team. But there are four in 'Do I really
have to work with these idiots?'

GAVIN BASKERVILLE

Take a leaf out of my book, and don't read under a tree
in autumn.

XAVIER MICHELIDES

Laziness walks in my family.

GAVIN BASKERVILLE

There's a saying, 'Opinions are like arseholes'. Well,
then, a lot of people I know are 'opinions'.

KARL CHANDLER

Time waits for no man. But it knows better than to ask
a woman to hurry up.

GAVIN BASKERVILLE

In space nobody can hear you scream. Because it's so
far away, I guess. It's pretty far.

ROB HUNTER

I opened up a box of chocolates and it wasn't like life at all. Forrest Gump is full of shit.

DAVE THORNTON

It's been said if you give a million chimpanzees a million typewriters, they'll eventually write the complete works of Shakespeare. So, was Shakespeare really a genius or just a guy with a lot of apes and office equipment?

BRUCE GRIFFITHS

Ladies: once you go black, you can never go back (to visit your racist parents).

KARL CHANDLER

Be careful what you wish for. It might come true. I really like boobs and now I have some.

DAVID TULK

Gee, I'm dreadful at staying focused on one thing at a

GERALDINE QUINN

A journey of a thousand miles begins with a refusal to ask for directions.

GAVIN BASKERVILLE

SCHOOL

There was a kid at my school who had an amazing
ability to do wee at any moment. If he was happy:
wee! If he was sad: wee! If he had to do wee: wee! And
the amazing thing was, if you caught him wetting his
pants, it used to look like a map of Nazi Germany
slowly invading Europe.

JUSTIN HAMILTON

When I was six, a kid at school dared me to shove a
Kool Mint up my arse. Desperate to be in the gang,
I did it. A little while later, he asked me how it felt.
I said it felt like a really big Tic Tac.

SAM SIMMONS

When I was in Year Five, this existentialist philosopher
came to speak to my class. After he left, all of us agreed
that if we live in a random and meaningless void,
then there's really no point learning how to play the
recorder.

JEFF HEWITT

I went to a really tough high school. You know
how every high school has a motto? Like Adelaide
Grammar has 'Aiming to be the Best', and Melbourne
Secondary's is 'Striving for Excellence'. My school's
was 'Because They're too Young for Prison'.

MICHAEL CONNELL

You have no idea how hard it is not to giggle when
you're a 13-year-old boy and your clarinet teacher
continuously compliments you on your fingering.

MICHAEL CHAMBERLIN

At high school I used to get picked on by this kid
called Shane. He used to stick a thumb tack on the
end of a pencil, rub it on the floor until it got hot from
friction, then give me a burn by sticking it on my neck.
I think he was the bully version of MacGyver.

MICHAEL CONNELL

I was teased at school for being fat, teased for being
poor, and teased about my family. It happens to a lot of
kids. And it really messes with your head if you were
homeschooled.

JACQUES BARRETT

My high school science teacher would always make us do that experiment where you put a coin into a glass of Coke. I'd put the coin in the glass, the Coke would slowly dissolve the coin, and my teacher would ask, 'What have you learned?' I'd say, 'Um, I should put my money in the bank, instead of a glass of Coke?'

MICHAEL CONNELL

I wasted so much time at school learning maths. Addition, subtraction, multiplication, pronouns, the whole lot. I've hardly used it since. I could count on one hand the eight times I've used it.

ADAM KEILY

I went to my high school reunion the other day. Well, sort of . . . I went to Centrelink.

MICHAEL CONNELL

I went to TAFE recently. I did a certificate III in Certificate Forgery.

MICHAEL WORKMAN

They're making philosophy degrees waterproof now. So you can shelter under them while you're begging for change.

MICHAEL WORKMAN

I went to a pretty crappy university. To give you an idea of how crappy my university was, in my last year there they ran a workshop called 'What is a Sentence?' I suppose they're improving, though. The year before they ran a workshop called 'What are a Sentence?'

MICHAEL CONNELL

How many uni students does it take to change a light bulb? When's it due in?

THE BEDROOM PHILOSOPHER

My parents sent me to a Christian 'gay conversion school' to try to turn me straight. It was a lot like any other quit-type meeting. On my first day I stood up and said, 'Hi, my name's Anthony Menchetti. I'm gay but I'm trying to quit. Down to one fag a day. Have one every morning with my coffee.'

ANTHONY MENCHETTI

SCIENCE

I was reading an article in a scientific journal recently. It was called 'Easy on the eye? Maybe also on the brain'. It was about how when human beings are around attractive objects, their brains function at a higher level. Which backs up what I've been saying all along. I was never dumb at school, my teachers were just ugly.

ANGUS HODGE

Sure, science can tell us how a bird flies, where it flies, when it flies and whether flying is right for us. But science cannot explain why. Oh, wait, it can. Go science!

MANFRED YON

A girl once told me, 'We can't be friends because you're a Virgo and I'm a Sagittarian.' No, we can't be friends because you're deluded. You believe gassy balls of plasma held together by gravity, millions of miles away actually control the minute intricacies of your personality. We can't be friends not because I was born in September and you were born in December, but because you own a dream catcher and you think it works.

MICHAEL CHAMBERLIN

I found out how important it is to separate your colours when you're doing laundry. I threw my camouflage pants in with the rest of the wash, and now I can't find anything.

KARL CHANDLER

People talk about solar power. Ever heard of something called 'clouds', genius? Ever hear of something called 'winter'? What's more – and I looked this up – the sun is over 93 million miles away! To put that in understandable terms, if the sun were a light bulb in China, the earth would be a basketball in Portugal. Does that sound like an efficient way to produce energy to you?

BEN POBJIE

I have a mood ring that supposedly changes colour to show what mood I'm in. Whenever I look at it, it reads 'sceptical'.

SAM BOWRING

SEX

I started chatting with a girl and somehow ended up
taking her home and sleeping with her. Afterwards
she told me she'd faked her orgasm and asked me if I
was upset. I told her, not really. I'd faked liking her as a
person so I could sleep with her.

JOHN CAMPBELL

I'm gay, but I prefer the term 'vagina decliner'.

ANTHONY MENCHETTI

How's this for a coincidence: my first car and my first
sexual partner were both old escorts.

TOM SIEGERT

I'm 23 and I still don't have my driver's licence. That
never really bothered me until I went to a singles party.
At the end of the night everybody threw their car keys
in a bowl, and I had to put my train ticket in there.
'Anyone for some sex in Werribee?' is not a good pick-
up line.

NICK CODY

My mum used to say, 'No one likes a girl who sleeps around.' I said, 'Well, someone must have liked her.'

DAVE O'NEIL

I read that a brothel in South Melbourne caught fire. So if you had a third-degree burns fetish, that would have been your time.

ADAM ROZENBACHS

I looked at my penis and noticed it had shrunk quite a lot. That's the last time I masturbate with Mum's anti-aging cream.

JONATHAN SCHUSTER

I want to invent the 'afternoon after' pill. It's going to be for those people who like to combine early starts with taking risks.

TOMMY LITTLE

I did a personality test once. It said that my three major characteristics were that I was intelligent, creative and highly sexual. Which means I'm just as comfortable taking on all comers in a diction competition as I am taking on all dicks in a coming competition.

YIANNI AGISILAOU

Tasmania wasn't the most ideal place to find out you're a little bit lesbian. And you do find out. I got a letter. 'Dear sir/madam.' That's all it said.

HANNAH GADSBY

I went out with a girl last night. We were in my room, trying to get it on. But I couldn't take her bra off. Then my dad walked in. He couldn't get it off either.

OLIVER PHOMMAVANH

I really don't like hookers. For starters, they make you wear a condom. Yeah, like *I'm* the dirty one.

LEHMO

I stayed in this motel with two single beds, just in case I picked up someone who didn't want to sleep with me.

DAVE O'NEIL

I got chlamydia once. The doctor told me not to worry as it affects 20 per cent of sexually active people between the ages of eighteen and 25. I wasn't worried, I just felt like I was inducted into a very odd gang. 'We won't mess you up right away, but in two weeks, it'll sting when you pee.'

NICK CODY

I once had sex with a model. I'll never do that again!
Those little plastic bits really hurt your penis.

LINDSAY WEBB

Guys often think that I would enjoy talking about
women with them because I am a lesbian. Just because
I am attracted to women, doesn't mean that I think
with my dick. It's made of rubber.

HANNAH GADSBY

A girlfriend once told me that making love to me was like
riding the rollercoaster at Dream World. Not too shabby,
I thought. Until she went on to say it's because, 'It goes
for two minutes and you feel a bit queasy afterwards. And
at the end you can buy photos of yourself that you didn't
know were being taken at the time.'

TROY KINNE

I lost my virginity to a 36-year-old woman wearing a
Yoda mask. I knew it was wrong at the time but, hey,
I really, really liked Yoda.

SAM SIMMONS

I went to bed with a schizophrenic once. To me that
counts as a threesome.

YIANNI AGISILAOU

When I was in Year Nine we started sex education. It made me so scared of getting a girl pregnant that the first party I went to, I wore a condom the whole night just in case.

TOMMY LITTLE

I haven't really had that much luck with the ladies. I think it's got a lot to do with the type of women I usually go for. You see, a lot of the girls I've dated in the past have been passive aggressive. When I slept with them, they were passive, but when they woke up, MAN, were they aggressive!

MIKEY MILEOS

Getting a beetroot stain on my bedspread reminds me of losing my virginity. Both have involved Sard Wonder Soap.

LOU SANZ

Apparently it's not uncommon for women to giggle uncontrollably after having an orgasm. I wouldn't know about this. Because I treat love making like show business, and always leave them wanting more. And there's no doubt that I leave my ladies really unsatisfied.

OLIVER CLARK

People love sex so much they want to do it every way they possibly can. But we don't do that with other things. For example, I like food. I like cake, but I never feel the need to sneak up on cake and pretend I'm robbing the place, dressed as Little Bo Peep who's lost her flock.

ALASDAIR TREMBLEY-BIRCHALL

I don't dance. Some people think they can tell how you are going to be in bed by your rhythm on the dance floor. So, what, your dance movies are like how you're supposed to be in bed, yeah? That's why I don't dance. I figure, stuff it. Ladies, you can find out the hard way.

DANIEL TOWNES

My wife and I had mirrored built-in robes installed in our bedroom. My mates said that'd be great because we could watch ourselves having sex. Yeah, that'd be great, if we were fit. But if you're not fit, you look in the mirrors and you don't see something sexy, what you see looks more like two pigs fighting over a stick of salami.

FABIEN CLARK

I saw a lady sculpting a clay baby with a pointy stick. Stupidly, without even thinking, I asked, 'Do pointy things make the best baby-making devices?'

JIMMY JAMES EATON

Vaginas are like the creatures in the movie *Gremlins*. If you get them wet and feed them after midnight, there's gonna be some mischief.

YIANNI AGISILAOU

I received a package with 'Do not bend' written on it. Either it's a packet of glowsticks, or someone sent me their erection.

MATT OKINE

My girlfriend doesn't think I'm very romantic because of what I did for her last Valentine's Day. You be the judge: as a special treat, I drank two litres of pineapple juice.

LEHMO

How good is KY Jelly? You could push your arm through a buttonhole with that stuff.

DANIEL TOWNES

I'm fascinated by those men who can just conjure up sex like wizards, the kind of guy you'd get if you crossed Gandalf with the Fonz. Actually, if you crossed Gandalf with the Fonz, you'd get a bloke in a leather jacket with a white beard and white robes going, 'You shall sit on it! Eeeeeyyyy.'

MICHAEL CHAMBERLIN

SPORT

I was really athletic at school. I played badminton.
Which is really intense. It's like tennis in *The Matrix*.

DAVE BLOUSTIEN

Ball boy is a task performed by children at the tennis.
It is also a name I would avoid if I was a superhero.

ROB HUNTER

The Melbourne Cup is called 'The race that stops a
nation'. Didn't the French call the Germans that in
1940?

DAVE THORNTON

Prime Minister Gillard says at the current rate of boat
people arrivals, it'd take 20 years to fill the MCG. It's
the same with North Melbourne supporters.

DANNY McGINLAY

Discus is just frisbee for people with no mates.

KARL CHANDLER

A friend once tried to convince me that cricket is a good sport by telling me, 'Nick, there were 96 000 people at the Boxing Day test. What do you think about that?' My response was, 'There were 250 000 people in the tsunami, but that doesn't make it good.'

NICK CODY

Outside the MCG, there should be a statue of Mitchell Johnson bowling a legside wide.

ADAM ROZENBACHS

I like cricket. I just barrack for the team wearing white. I haven't lost yet.

DAVE THORNTON

I played golf as a kid because according to my mum, 'netball is for sluts'.

HANNAH GADSBY

I played in a social mixed netball team in a league where you get to name your own team. We called ourselves 'BYE round'. So when our opponents read their weekly roster, they thought, 'Sweet, we've got the week off.'

BEN DARSOW

I'm running in this year's marathon. My main motivation is that I'm doing it for charity. And I'm hoping to raise awareness for chafing.

PETE SHARKEY

I wanted to take up a sport and it was going to be either lawn bowling or Aussie Rules football. I decided that footy is for pussies. How many World War Two vets you got playing in your local footy team? Probably none. Well, there's six at my lawn bowls club.

TOMMY LITTLE

I was watching a boxing match on TV with Anthony Mundine. The commentator introduced him as Anthony 'The Man' Mundine. I wondered why he chose that nickname? Maybe there were a number of female boxers also called 'Anthony Mundine', and he was trying to clear up any confusion.

JOHN CAMPBELL

There's a certain swimming stroke that I don't understand how it got its name. The butterfly stoke. I understand that the movement is a bit like wings, but lots of things have wings! Things that are better at going in a straight line than a frickin' butterfly. I just think if we're going to call it the butterfly stroke, there needs to be something a little more butterfly-esque about it. Like maybe when the starter pistol goes off, everyone has to jump out of a sleeping bag.

SAM BOWRING

I'm not into golf. If I wanted to stroll and interrupt it by sharply twisting my body, I'd walk along a nudist beach.

DAVE THORNTON

I don't understand all these people who do marathons for charity, and ask you to donate money to the charity to support them for the run. For example, I have a friend who does the 'Run for Refugees'. But what the heck does running do for refugees? Isn't running what caused the problem in the first place? You're not helping. Just give them the money!

RONNY CHIENG

TECHNOLOGY

I believe we would save a lot of time in the shower if there was just a tap labelled 'warm'.

ROB HUNTER

An iPhone is like a penis. It's fun to play with when you're on your own but it's rude to pull it out at the dinner table.

TOM GLEESON

I don't like the iPhone app that tells you where booze buses are. I think it's irresponsible to use your phone while drink driving.

ADAM ROZENBACHS

I gave my dad a GPS. He loves it. Now I don't have the heart to tell him it's actually an old Nokia 6210 with Snake.

JASON PESTELL

Wikipedia is just like a bunch of Fantales, but with no lollies.

KARL CHANDLER

I hate predictive text, what next? Predictive speak?
Your friend will ask you . . . 'Hey, Jimmy, how you
doing?' And you'll reply, 'I'm really . . . hood . . .
home . . . gone . . . goof . . . GOOD, thanks!'

JIMMY JAMES EATON

I got a new phone. First thing it did was text an ex-
boyfriend. We're going to get on just fine.

LOU SANZ

If you type 'lazy' in predictive text it spells 'jazz'.
Coincidence?

JOSH EARL

I'm currently taking an Arabic language class. I didn't
want to, it's just that somebody changed the language
on my mobile phone and I can't get it back.

MICHAEL CHAMBERLIN

I think my calculator is autistic because it's really good
with numbers but not so good in social situations.
I mean, it says HELLO but after that, it just wants to
talk about BOOBS and SEASHELLS.

ALISON BICE

The other day I got four strikes in a row on Wii Bowling, and I thought, 'This is the BEST DAY OF MY LIFE!' Then I looked at my little boy, smiling up at me, and I thought, good God, what am I thinking? Where are my priorities? That's when I realised the best day of my life was actually when I beat him at Wii Boxing.

BEN POBJIE

There are video games that are designed to keep you fit. Isn't that a contradiction in terms? It's like using heroin to get your life back on track.

MARK TRENWITH

If you suspect that your partner is a sexual deviant and you want to find out for sure, go to their laptop and look at 'internet history'. If there isn't one, they are one. After a session, all of us deviants delete history, remove cookies, empty cache, clear Real Player Downloader, Windex the screen and keyboard, destroy the laptop, change your username and run, run! The federal police are coming!

LAWRENCE MOONEY

I got busted for plagiarism at uni. The teacher said that I copied my essay straight off the internet. It's a bit hard to talk your way out of that kind of thing when halfway down the first page of your essay it says, 'Click Here For More Information'.

RAY BADRAN

I don't understand what it means when Twitter is 'over capacity'. Too many people eating too many sandwiches?

TOMMY DASSALO

Today my computer crashed and then informed me that it'd had an 'unknown error'. That's pretty vague, for a think machine. People can't get away with that kind of shit. If I go down the shops specifically to buy milk, and when I get back home I don't have any milk, I don't say, 'Well, must have been an unknown error.' No. I know what I did wrong. But, in my defence, that butterfly was asking to be chased.

SAM BOWRING

We can put a man on the moon, with one jab of a needle we can prevent diseases that in the past killed millions of people, we can create human life in a test tube. Yet what's the most talked about technological achievement? A website where friends who are already friends can ask their friends if they can be friends.

MICHAEL CHAMBERLIN

eBay outbidding helps people with the same taste to despise each other.

STEELE SAUNDERS

A study found that the iPads on display in shops can contain up to 18 times more harmful germs than the flush handle in a men's toilet. I find this hard to believe. I've never met a man who's ever flushed a public toilet.

ADAM KEILY

What came first: the idea for the light bulb, or the idea for the idea for the light bulb?

JOSH EARL

True story: the police received a 000 call from a man in Pakenham because his GPS had run out of batteries. The response should've been, 'Certainly, sir, we'll immediately send an officer out to shoot you, so that you can call us back with an actual emergency.'

MATT ELSBURY

I thought I had one of those awesome 3D TVs. Turns out I didn't. I've just been stoned for 11 years. In fact, I don't even have a TV. It's a window.

DAVID TULK

I once set my GPS to direct me to Sydney, then drove
to Adelaide. I wanted to see if I could make the GPS
lose its temper.

MATT ELSBURY

TRANSPORT

I need a bike. Not because I like riding, I just think I'll get abused less for walking around in Lycra if I have a bike with me.

TOMMY LITTLE

I was flying back from Melbourne. As the plane came into Sydney, the stewardess made an announcement: 'Ladies and gentlemen, in preparation for landing, the pilot has turned on the "fasten your seatbelt" sign.' I put up my hand and suggested that he also lower the wheels.

BRUCE GRIFFITHS

I'm so post-modern, I bought my own skywriting bi-plane and crashed accidentally while writing my suicide note.

THE BEDROOM PHILOSOPHER (from 'I'm So Post-modern')

I was boarding an army Hercules in Basra, and it's a lot like boarding a normal flight. You check in your main luggage and carry your hand luggage. Then your hand luggage has to go through an X-ray machine. I'm in the queue, and in front of me soldiers are putting through guns, ammo, hand grenades, and I'm thinking, 'What are you looking for?' I was waiting to get to the other side, when they pull out my nail clippers and say, 'Not with these, mate.'

LEHMO

The installation of full-body scanners in airports has on one hand outraged the average traveller, but on the other hand made clearing airport security a thrill for your average flasher.

MAT KENNEALLY

I booked a ticket on the Concorde. I thought, 'Cool, a plane that travels faster than sound.' It had taken off before I heard the boarding announcement.

BRUCE GRIFFITHS

You know you're about to do a long-haul flight when you're taking every possible opportunity to fart while you still can.

JASON CHONG

My first time flying, I remember looking out the window and thinking, 'Those people look just like ants.' Moments later, we touched down on the Island of the Ant People.

BRUCE GRIFFITHS

I want to own a ship and call it the S.S. Stutter.

JOSH EARL

I was on a tram the other day and I was listening in on a couple's conversation about how rude eavesdropping is. I leant over between the two and said, 'I tend to agree.'

TOM SIEGERT

Volkswagen named one of their cars 'Golf'. Why would you name a car after a sport that's slow, expensive and the hardest part is driving?

DAVE THORNTON

I was in a taxi and I think it's about time we started adding some new questions to the cabdrivers test. Like 'What is soap?'

DAVO

I heard they're making a car that runs on water. I'm not looking forward to that. Petrol costs a dollar forty a litre. Have you ever bought water from a petrol station? Half a litre of Mount Franklin costs you three dollars! I'm not made of cash, you know.

DAVE THORNTON

I failed my driving test the first time that I took it.
I failed because the instructor directed me down the
street that my ex-boyfriend lives on. And apparently
they take points off you if you accelerate towards
pedestrians.

LAURA DAVIS

TV

TV

Television is a very powerful tool. But then again, so is
Eddie McGuire.

GREG FLEET

I love performing stand-up comedy, mainly because I can't
stand staying at home and watching Australian television.
Because it's just so out of touch with reality. *All Saints*
was one of the most popular shows on Australian TV.
How can a show that is entirely based around a hospital
have no brown or Asian doctors? If you ever wake up in
hospital, and there are no brown or Asian doctors, get out
of there. You're not in a hospital. You're on the set of a
mediocre but well-loved Australian TV series.

NAZEEM HUSSAIN

I love it on *So You Think You Can Dance* when they get
voted out. They always say, 'You haven't seen the last of
me.' Trust me, you're a dancer, we have.

MICHAEL CHAMBERLIN

I was watching an episode of *Huey's Cooking
Adventures*. I was expecting some magical journey, but

the fat prick never left his kitchen. Standing in your kitchen getting obese doesn't constitute an adventure. If they ever made a theme park ride at Adventure World, 'Huey's Gradual Descent Into Heart Disease' would not be a crowd favourite.

JOHN CAMPBELL

I'm a racist to racists. I'm like the Dexter of racists.

ASHER TRELEAVEN

There's a New Zealand version of *The Apprentice*. Each week, you find out which contestant will move to Melbourne.

STEELE SAUNDERS

Was anyone surprised Fox Mulder and Dana Scully never solved anything? What sort of filing system is putting everything under X?

BRUCE GRIFFITHS

We don't have celebrities in this country, we have personalities. All you have to do in Australia is jump up and down in front of the *Sunrise* window for a week and you'll be on next season's *Dancing with the Stars*.

BEN ELLWOOD

Lost was a very racist show to Australians. It's about a plane leaving Sydney to Los Angeles, with apparently only two Australians on board! The pregnant lady and one of the flight attendants. They need to explain what happened to the other Aussies. A flashback to when the plane crashes on the island and all the Australians are flung to the other side of the island. Then two days later the United Nations rock up, saying, 'Shhh! Get on the rescue plane.' The Aussies say, 'Thanks, mate, but by the way, there are some yanks on the other side.' 'Shut up! We know! Bugger 'em!'

DANNY McGINLAY

People's complaints about *The Simpsons* aren't as good as they used to be.

KARL CHANDLER

Whose decision was it to give the yellow costume to the only Asian Power Ranger?

JASON CHATFIELD

Totally Wild has a segment called 'What Scat is That?' It's exactly what you think. Especially if you're thinking, 'Wow. Awesome.'

JASON CHONG

I watched a lot of *Inspector Gadget* when I was a kid. So whenever someone asked me to pull their finger, I got scared. Because I thought they might turn into a helicopter.

BART FREEBAIRN

Border Security should be called *Asians Smuggling Lizards (White People Apparently Never Commit Crimes)*.

MICHAEL CHAMBERLIN

As I get older, I find that when I watch *MasterChef*, I make the same noises as if I were watching porn.

TROY KINNE

Seeing someone with a rat's tail is like watching an episode of *Lost* halfway into the season. I'm confused and I just want to know what's wrong.

RHYS NICHOLSON

CSI only has two storylines: the episode where someone 'has a secret', and the episode where 'it's one of their own'. The only exception is the special two-hour finale, when 'one of their own has a secret'.

STEELE SAUNDERS

I saw one of those terrorist propaganda videos on the news. This one featured a 'suicide bomber graduation ceremony'. There's a school for suicide bombers! And I'm guessing the five-year reunion won't be well attended.

CHRIS NORTH

I saw a guy on *The Biggest Loser* saying, 'I'm doing this for my kids.' Dude, when your kid's friends watch you on national television attempting to run 15 metres before collapsing and sobbing into your fat tits, your kids are gonna get the living shit kicked out of them.

BEN ELLWOOD

Watching TV, I notice there seems to be a growing amount of smutty 'SMS Flirt' and '1800 Hot Babe' type advertisements. The worst one I saw was called 'Dateline' with George Negus. I watched the whole thing, and the son of a bitch didn't even take his glasses off.

JOHN CAMPBELL

When I watch TV and see a character also watching TV, I feel like a babushka doll of laziness.

JIMMY JAMES EATON

I think some car ads can be misleading. Especially the way they advertise the number of doors. They'll say, 'Drive away with this five-door sedan,' or 'Check out this three-door hatch.' Sorry, but I've never ever seen anyone enter the car via the boot. So let's quit calling the boot a door.

PETE SHARKEY

In the ad for Pine O Cleen wipes, they say, 'Fact: we even kill girl germs.' That's crap. That stuff does nothing for my thrush.

GERALDINE HICKEY

I find those World Vision ads odd. The ones that show a child and say, 'This is Rahasia. She is four years old. She lives in a house made out of two pieces of corrugated iron. If she wants to get a drink, she has to walk for four hours to reach the nearest water pump.' Why doesn't she just move the pieces of iron closer to the water pump?

TONY BESSELINK

Why do they sell gym equipment and self-improvement products on TV at 3 a.m.? If you're up at 3 a.m., health is obviously not your top priority.

PETE SHARKEY

People say you shouldn't let your kids watch too much TV because they might try to imitate the things they see. I can't remember this affecting me. Except one time after watching *Star Wars*, I beat the shit out of a kid having an asthma attack because I thought he was turning to the dark side.

FABIEN CLARK

How do you stop terrorism? Give them all free cable TV. Would terrorists willingly blow themselves up if they knew they wouldn't find out what happened next to Don Draper?

JUSTIN HAMILTON

WOMEN

I don't understand why girls use exfoliant. I've never looked at a girl and thought, 'Oh, she'd be hot, but *way* too much skin. She should scrub off a few layers.'

MICHAEL CONNELL

When I first met my girlfriend, she was wearing glasses. This was a big thing for me. Not because she looked smart and sexy, but because her poor eyesight might mean I'd be in with a chance.

STEELE SAUNDERS

Women don't look and me and think, 'I want to have sex with Michael.' Women look at me and think, 'I wouldn't mind getting a lift home from Michael. Because he won't try anything.'

MICHAEL CHAMBERLIN

As a woman, if you think your arse looks big in that dress, it's probably just your insecurities talking. Your Big. Fat. Insecurities.

ALISON BICE

A friend asked me what my favourite thing about her was. I said, 'Can you smile again for me?' She smiled, and then I said, 'Your hair.'

JONATHAN SCHUSTER

What's with all these questions girls ask at the start? They want to know everything. Who are you? What are you doing? Is that a camera?

OLIVER PHOMMAVANH

I tried one of those new 'invisible bras'. It works. It's disappeared, along with my support.

LOU SANZ

I was chatting this girl up in a pub and she actually stopped me in mid-conversation, pointed to her body and said, 'Mate! You wouldn't know what to do with all this even if you did get it home!' I just said, 'Why? Were you made by IKEA?'

JON BROOKS

Women love a man with a sense of humour. But not comedians. It's like saying, 'Women love a man with a big penis. But not two-feet long.'

YIANNI AGISILAOU

I'm a retrosexual. I'm attracted to women who looked good in the seventies and eighties. To me they represent good times, and great classic hits.

JEFF HEWITT

Girls have high expectations. You want a friend, a lover, a provider. Just pick one.

OLIVER PHOMMAVANH

I'm tired of women who eat a piece of chocolate then spend the next three hours telling me how 'naughty' they are. Having sex with a bloke in an alleyway three minutes after you meet him . . . that is naughty. And awesome. One piece of 'Fruit and Nut'? Not so naughty.

MICHAEL CHAMBERLIN

Some girls say they find it hard to get into comedy, and I think that's wrong. I think they have it easy. A funny female comedian friend of mine does this joke about how she thinks her breasts are not big enough and then says she sees girls half her age with bigger breasts. She does it in a way that gets a big laugh, which is fine. But if I were to do that joke about my small penis, and I said, 'I see boys half my age with bigger penises,' I'd be doing this gig from jail.

STEELE SAUNDERS

I like to tease babies by getting my breasts out. Now
they know how I feel when my housemate leaves an
empty carton of milk in the fridge.

ALISON BICE

Two women having sex without a man is like having
a lounge room without a television. Most men will
never be able to understand it, but you can entertain
yourself.

HANNAH GADSBY

I robbed an old lady. It's pretty easy if you've never
done it. You just walk up next to her, snatch her bag
and run! However, unfortunately I snatched her
colostomy bag by mistake. So you can imagine my
surprise when I opened it up to actually find her purse
in there.

OLIVER CLARK

My hormones played a cruel joke on me when they
gave me childbearing hips. 'Let's make this one
into the ultimate baby-making vessel and then give
her absolutely no desire to make one.' I'm like a
Transformer that doesn't fancy driving.

HANNAH GADSBY

I just saw a pregnant lady pushing an empty pram.
Too soon ...

MATT OKINE

In high school I had a crush on a girl for four years,
and when I finally built up the courage to ask her out,
she was like, 'Over my dead body.' Which I think was
harsh. Anyway, I found out recently that she was killed
in a horrible, horrible car accident, so I guess now,
technically, we're dating.

MIKEY MILEOS

WORK

I wasn't always a comedian. Originally I was a dog trainer at an obedience school. But I was fired for having an affair with a student.

DAVE JORY

I applied for a job as a waiter and had to go to a job interview. One of the questions was, 'How serious are you about becoming a waiter?' I would go so far as to say absolutely no one *wants* to be a waiter. No one's going up to their career counsellor saying, 'I'm looking for a job where I get absolutely no respect, where I get to hear people complaining all the time, and to top it all off I want to be paid fuck-all.'

TONY BESSELINK

I think it's a great Australian tradition to hate your boss. I'm a comedian, I'm self-employed, and even I hate my boss. He's rude, he makes me work long hours and every now and then, he tries to grab my cock.

MICHAEL CHAMBERLIN

I hate being unemployed. The only thing that suits me
is the hours.

DEAN EIZENBERG

When someone says, 'Pull your finger out,' it usually
means 'get to work', unless you're a proctologist. Then
it means, 'Time to knock off.'

SAM BOWRING

I used to work in a supermarket, and I hated it. I once
had this supervisor go mental at me for not being
productive enough. I just said, 'Hey, I'm a casual
worker. Says it right there on my payslip.'

BEN DARSOW

I worked at KFC for three years, which is a long time.
My plan was to work my way up the ranks and make
Colonel. But that old bastard just won't retire.

DAVE JORY

Acting is not a game. Twister, Monopoly, Hungry
Hungry Hippos: these are games. Acting is not
Twister. Unless it stars Helen Hunt and Bill Paxton.
And even then it's debatable.

CHARLES BARRINGTON

To improve their image, boring accountants need their own TV show. They could call it *Bondi Accountant* or *Accountant Wants a Wife*. Or *So You Think You Can Add*.

LEHMO

How did Mr Snooze become Captain? How can you even become captain of a bedding store? He must've slept his way to the top.

JONATHAN SCHUSTER

When I was a naughty child, my mother used to say, 'If you don't get it together, you're going to wind up a garbage man for the rest of your life.' Garbage men can earn over $100K a year. If she had any foresight, she would have said, 'If you don't get it together, you're going to wind up a burnt-out, drug-addicted stand-up comic, begging for the approval of strangers and peddling yuk yuks for drink tokens.'

BEN ELLWOOD

I applied to be an actor in pornographic movies. They said they'll let me know when they have an opening for me. But I may have to start at the bottom.

DAVE JORY

I want to be a taxi driver. Just for the company car.

PETE SHARKEY

I tell you what, if you're a bomb-disposal expert, and you wake up, you put your uniform on, and off you go to work, then please, please make sure that you get to the bus stop on time. Because people really don't want to see you chasing after a bus.

SAM BOWRING

Acting is the second oldest profession in the world. If you would like to know the first oldest . . . ask your mother.

CHARLES BARRINGTON

We have a cleaner who comes fortnightly and I'm not particularly comfortable with the whole servant thing. The people-cleaning-up-after-me-type relationship always seems very condescending to me, especially when it comes time to pay. I don't know whether to hand the money to her, leave it on the bench and point to it, or hide it under a cushion so it's a nice surprise as she's cleaning up.

LAWRENCE MOONEY

I was, briefly, a teacher. This taught me two things.
One: I hate children. Two: the cricket bat is an
underused educational tool. After all, an unconscious
child is a quiet child.

MATT ELSBURY

I went into an office and they had one of those
motivational posters up on the wall. It read, 'Aim
for the moon. Then even if you miss, you'll still land
among the stars'. I thought it was nice. I just bet it's
not up on the wall at the NASA space institute. Their
poster would probably just say, 'Aim for the moon:
Astronauts have families'.

LAURA DAVIS

I think a staple is just a paperclip that's committed.

PETE SHARKEY

I just found out what NSFW stands for. I also just got
fired.

MATT OKINE

Recently I've been working at a henna tattoo parlour.
But now I'm looking for something more permanent.

DAVE JORY

When I used to go to work at the supermarket I would become dumb. I would swipe on, and my brain would swipe off. I remember serving women who would walk up to the counter and place three items down directly in front of me, and I'd say, 'Hi, how are you?' and they'd say, 'Tampons, Panadol, and a kilo of chocolate . . . Fill in the gaps, dickhead.'

BEN DARSOW

I wouldn't get a tattoo from someone who is covered in them, because business must be slow.

DANIEL TOWNES

There's an unwritten agreement when you go to a hairdresser. You tell them how you want your hair to be cut, they ignore those instructions, do whatever the hell they want, then you walk out depressed while they giggle and point.

MICHAEL CHAMBERLIN

I always get confused between podiatrists and pediatricians. All I know is: one of them has sex with kids.

TOM BALLARD

THE WORLD

I landed at the Auckland airport, and decided to go to the tourist information booth. I said to the guy in the booth, 'I've never been to Auckland before. What should I go see while I'm here?' He goes, 'Um ... *The Matrix*?'

MICHAEL CONNELL

I visited the Coliseum in Rome. They told me in its peak it held 50 000 spectators. I thought, 'Man, because they used roman numerals, how hard would it be to find your seat?'

DAVE THORNTON

Rome wasn't built in a day? No joke, it's still not finished.

DANIEL TOWNES

I want to go to Italy. I think it'd be like an Italian restaurant but bigger.

DAVE THORNTON

If I went to Amsterdam, I'd visit the orange-light district. Because I like to take things slow.

MIKEY MILEOS

I can only assume that Amsterdam has the world's best Cash Converters.

STEELE SAUNDERS

I'm a Scottish-born French-Canadian Australian. I'm looking for a Scottish-born French-Canadian Australian lady to breed with, to try to keep the bloodline pure.

ALASDAIR TREMBLEY-BIRCHALL

I am a British and Australian citizen. I prefer living in Australia, though. So in UK elections I vote BNP just to keep people like me out of Britain.

DANNY McGINLAY

I went over to England to do comedy and they didn't get my accent at all. They said, 'Hey, mate, speak slower.' If I spoke any slower, I'd be spelling.

DANIEL TOWNES

Some people are quite unfair on Americans. I've only met one truly stupid one. I asked who his favourite president was, and he said Lincoln. I asked him why, and he said, 'Because Abraham Lincoln was born in a log cabin that he built with his bare hands!'

DANNY McGINLAY

I don't think Irish people realise just how sexy their accent is. It's like airborne Rohypnol.

CELIA PACQUOLA

When travelling through the US, I stayed in a town called Camden, which is in New Jersey. Camden has the highest murder rate in the world per capita, but is ranked seventeenth for muggings. I don't like any place where my wallet is safer than my life.

NICK CODY

I studied Japanese for six years. I learned one phrase, '*Wakarimasen*'. That means, 'I don't understand'.

MICHAEL CONNELL

Americans spell colour, 'color'. It's a country where the children were struggling with spelling, so instead of making the teaching better, they made the language easier.

YIANNI AGISILAOU

I do gigs in the Middle East for the troops, and they're always really good shows. Because when the hecklers have guns, you bring your 'A' game.

LEHMO

On the issue of whaling, I side with the Japanese.
You've all read *Mr Archimedes' Bath*? With global
warming, the sea levels are rising. Does it not make
sense to take the giant, fat animals out of it? Whales
are killing the planet and Japan is the only country
with the balls to do anything about it.

SIMON GODFREY

In the US, I stayed in a suburb of Brooklyn called
Bedford-Stuyvesant. Here's a tip, if you can learn more
about a suburb from rap music than a Lonely Planet
guide, don't go.

NICK CODY

I'm troubled by the idea that my cool Adidas runners
might be made by an exploited, underprivileged
eight-year-old child somewhere in Asia. Troubled
and amazed! An eight-year-old making runners is
an awesome achievement. But child labour is wrong
and one day I would like to open a footwear factory
in the first world staffed purely by underprivileged
children who can make runners and raise money for
underprivileged children working in the third-world
factories.

LAWRENCE MOONEY

I heard in China they use over 4000 characters in their writing system. I heard that and thought, 'Man, one Chinese computer keyboard must take up at least two floors.'

DAVE THORNTON

I'm no longer welcome in Thailand. I misunderstood when one of the locals asked if I wanted to take part in a cockfight. For the record, I lost. But to be fair, I wasn't even expecting her to have a cock.

TOM SIEGERT

I'd like to be granted whatever superpower I want for one day. I'd choose China.

SIMON GODFREY

In Montreal they're all bilingual. That's impressive. I'm an Australian and I'm barely lingual.

DAVE THORNTON

I purchased an old Indian burial ground. I'm going to build a house on it. Hopefully this decision doesn't come back to haunt me.

CHARLES BARRINGTON

Why do armies persist with the obstacle course? When in the history of war has a country's last line of defence been monkey bars and two rows of tyres?

BRUCE GRIFFITHS

I sat on my globe, and now it's a map.

KARL CHANDLER

I bought a voodoo world map. I put pins in all the countries I don't like.

CHARLES BARRINGTON

My opinion on climate change depends on the evidence that I see. So if an attractive girl believes in climate change, so do I.

OLIVER PHOMMAVANH

I got a letter from my sponsor child recently. I also got a little picture, but the most disturbing thing was he'd written that when he grew up, he wanted to become an artist. I read that, then looked at the picture and thought, 'My God. These payments are never going to stop.'

GERALDINE HICKEY

BIOGRAPHIES

YIANNI AGISILAOU

Yianni Agisilaou is a UK-based Australian comedian who has a growing fan base in London. He has performed at comedy festivals worldwide, including Edinburgh, Melbourne, Amsterdam, Johannesburg, Leicester and Reading. He loves cosmology, Scrabble and human interactions.

YIANNI.ORG
TWITTER.COM/YIANNI_A

RAY BADRAN

Ray attended university, completing a Bachelor of Medical Science in only twice the allocated time. After quitting and getting fired from a number of jobs (nine in total), Ray decided to try his hand at stand-up comedy. His hand liked comedy and so did the rest of his body, so he continued to perform it.

RAYBADRAN.COM

TOM BALLARD

Tom Ballard's level of success for his age regularly annoys his peers, but what they don't know is he steals all his jokes from old Punky Brewster scripts. Tom is co-host of the triple j breakfast show and won Best Newcomer at the 2009 Melbourne International Comedy Festival. He highly recommends swearing and cheap callbacks as shortcuts to laughter.

TOMBALLARD.COM.AU
TWITTER.COM/TOMCBALLARD

JACQUES BARRETT

On the forefront of Sydney's rapidly expanding comedy scene, Jacques is among a talented bunch of rising Australian stars whose unique brand of performance takes a crowd on a journey they never thought possible.

TWITTER.COM/JACQUESBARRETT

CHARLES BARRINGTON

A household name in the world of theatre and his house, Charles Barrington is the actor's actor's actor and gentleman's gentleman. Regarded as one of the most persistent actors of his generation, the raconteur and beekeeper is always ready to dish the dirt and dirty the dishes on all of his former acting friends and colleagues.

TWITTER.COM/BARRINGTONJAM

GAVIN BASKERVILLE

Since 1999 Gavin has performed around Australia at comedy rooms, major festivals and corporate events. He has written and performed for TV and radio, regularly hosts professional stand-up shows and runs a number of comedy courses around the country.

GAVINBASKERVILLE.COM
TWITTER.COM/GBASKERVILLE

THE BEDROOM PHILOSOPHER

The Bedroom Philosopher ('Beddy Phil') is a veteran of the Australian club scene, winning Red Faces in 1984 with 'Bitch', a parody of Chris Franklin's 'Bloke'. He is best known for his concept album *Songs From The 86 Tram*, which reached #2 on Nova's Coldest 100, and was described by US tastemakers Pitchfork as 'disc missing'. He is survived by his girlfriend.

BEDROOMPHILOSOPHER.COM

TONY BESSELINK

Tony Besselink was born in 1988 (i.e., he's 23). He's a uni student (i.e., unemployed), performs comedy around Melbourne (i.e., the place with the tall buildings) and likes to play games on his computer (i.e., he's single). He likes comedy based on abstract concepts and ideas (i.e., try not to get stuck with him at parties).

ALISON BICE

Alison Bice is famous. You should definitely know who she is. She had five lines in ABC's *The Librarians*. She also made appearances on *Stand Up Australia* for The Comedy Channel. Bice spent over a year performing comedy in the UK, where she made headlines stealing jokes from Jordan Paris on *Britain's Got Talent*.

TWITTER.COM/ALISONBICE

DAVE BLOUSTIEN

Dave is a multi-award-winning comedy writer for *Good News Week* and *The Glass House*, international stand-up comedian, improviser and published academic. He's been forced to defend his comedy in a court of law and won. Twice.

BLOUSTIEN.COM
TWITTER.COM/DAVEBLOUSTIEN

SAM BOWRING

Sam began performing stand-up comedy at the age of sixteen. Since then he has been nominated for various impressive awards, though he's never actually won anything. He's also written books, plays, and for various televisual broadcasts. For more details about this fascinating yet humble genius, visit his website.

SAMBOWRING.COM

HARLEY BREEN

Harley is one of the country's best respected stand-up comedians. In 2010 he was named Spleen Comic of the Year, and at the 2011 Melbourne International Comedy Festival Breen won the Piece of Wood (Comics' Choice Award).

TWITTER.COM/HARLEYBREEN

JON BROOKS

Jon Brooks is a former journalist and political staffer turned comedian. He's been performing since 2008 and is generally just a whinging lefty. Based in Adelaide, he's also the drummer in Adelaide punk/metal band The Guantanamo Bay City Rollers.

TWITTER.COM/BOGANS_HEROES

PAUL CALLEJA

Paul Calleja is a comedian and writer and has appeared on *Rove*, *Headliners* and *Hey Hey it's Saturday*. He also has a long list of TV writing credits, including *Jimeoin*, *Rove*, *Before the Game* and *skitHOUSE*. His material follows a reasonable logic to bizarre conclusions. Hilariously deadpan.

TWITTER.COM/PCALLEJA1

JOHN 'CAMBO' CAMPBELL

John 'Cambo' Campbell is a writer and comedian. He is known for his unique 'comedy noir' style of stand-up, but also performs as one half of sketch duo 'Luke and Cambo.' Cambo writes and performs on Channel 31's *Studio A*.

MICHAEL CHAMBERLIN

Stand-up comedian, writer, Australia's worst actor, left hander, coeliac, Hawthorn supporter, atheist, brunette, fingernail biter, castrato, Best First Year Player St Mary's Amateur Football Club 1999, son, brother, uncle, cousin, nephew, brother in law and cider drinker.

MICHAELCHAMBERLIN.COM.AU
TWITTER.COM/CHAMBERLINM

KARL CHANDLER

He put this book together. His bio is somewhere else. Don't make me write it all out again.

KARLCHANDLER.COM
TWITTER.COM/KARLCHANDLER

JASON CHATFIELD

Jason Chatfield is the fifth cartoonist to write and draw the popular Australian comic strip 'Ginger Meggs', which appears in 34 countries. He writes over 380 gags a year. They're okay sometimes. He enjoys writing in the third person, and is widely thought to have invented the sandwich.

JASONCHATFIELD.COM/
TWITTER.COM/JASONIUM

RONNY CHIENG

Ronny Chieng is Chinese, born in Johor Bahru, Malaysia, raised in New Hampshire, MA US and Singapore. He graduated from the University of Melbourne Law School in 2009. He was national runner-up in the Melbourne International Comedy Festival Raw Comedy competition in 2010.

RONNYCHIENG.COM
TWITTER.COM/RONNYCHIENG

JASON CHONG

Jason Chong has done lots of radio and some TV, as well as performing many times at the Adelaide Fringe, a few times at the Melbourne International Comedy Festival and once at the Edinburgh Fringe.

JASONCHONG.COM.AU
TWITTER.COM/JASONCHONGCOMIC

FABIEN CLARK

Fabien Clark is the type of comedian who will make you feel like there's always someone worse off than you. He is married with three kids, has a dead-end job and is based in Adelaide. His tears are your joy.

OLIVER CLARK

Wearing blue velvet, white loafers, gold cufflinks, and a smile that's all cheese, Oliver Clark is one gentleman who has brought the Razzle and the Dazzle to Australian stand-up comedy. A consummate entertainer, worthy of playing Vegas.

TWITTER.COM/THEOLIVERCLARK

THE CLOUD GIRLS

Madeleine Culp and Jennifer Carnovale are a comedy duo aka 'Carnovale and Culp', or 'The Cloud Girls'. We do stand-up, comedy and fringe festivals and are radio presenters on Triple J. We won a rubber chicken at the Sydney Comedy Festival in 2010 for being Best Newcomers. Best chicken we've won so far!

CARNOVALEANDCULP.COM
TWITTER.COM/CARNOVALECULP

NICK CODY

With his unique blend of brutally honest and self-deprecating humour, Nick Cody has already supported some of Australia's biggest comedy names, performed stand-up on Dave Hughes' DVD and been a permanent cast member of Channel 31's *Studio A*.

TWITTER.COM/THENICKCODY

DANIEL CONNELL

Daniel Connell made his comedy debut in the 2008 Green Faces competition, where it was apparent that this lad from Batemans Bay had a talent for laid-back Australian humour. Now based in Melbourne, he is a regular on the local scene.

TWITTER.COM/DANIELCONNELL3

MICHAEL CONNELL

Known for routines that are both clean and high impact, Michael's comedy has met with critical and popular acclaim. His ability to entertain any crowd ensures Michael is in constant demand as a performer at corporate events, charity functions, universities and all of Australia's best comedy clubs.

MICHAELCONNELL.COM.AU
TWITTER.COM/MICHAELRCONNELL

JOEL CREASEY

Joel is one of Australia's youngest, brightest and most sought-after comedians, cutting a swathe through the Australian comedy scene with his fast-paced wit, up-to-the-minute material and engaging delivery.

TWITTER.COM/JOELCREASEY

BEN DARSOW

Ben Darsow is one of Australia's most refreshing touring comedians. He delivers a free-flowing observational style of social commentary that brings light to a diverse range of universal topics relevant to modern-day life. Ben does this with insight, intelligence and a sense of playfulness that is never far from the surface.

BENDARSOW.COM

TOMMY DASSALO

Combining masterful storytelling with stand-up comedy, Tommy Dassalo is a unique young talent. He has appeared on *The Librarians*, written jokes for *Rove, Talkin' 'Bout Your Generation* and *TV Burp*, and toured to comedy festivals around Australia, where he is a regular favourite of critics and punters alike.

TOMMYDASSALO.COM
TWITTER.COM/DASSALO

LAURA DAVIS

Laura Davis is from Perth, WA. She started her comedy career at the age of nineteen as part of the Triple J Raw Comedy competition. Where science meets surrealism, Laura's comedy is playful, improvised, interactive and exuberant.

DAVO

Davo was only nineteen years old when he made his first national TV appearance in 2000. It was only recently that he caused an uproar on NBC's *Last Comic Standing* after he walked off the show during a dispute with the judges over his knock-knock joke.

DAVOCOMEDY.COM

JACK DRUCE

Originally from Canada, Jack started stand-up at the ripe old age of fifteen. Since then he's been the youngest person to put on a Melbourne International Comedy Festival show, and the oldest person to enjoy SpongeBob SquarePants without being ironic.

JACKDRUCE.COM
TWITTER.COM/JACKDRUCE

JOSH EARL

Josh Earl is a Melbourne comedian who has performed extensively around Australia and the world with sell-out shows in some of the world's largest festivals. He hosts a popular sketch radio show on 3RRR FM called 'Lime Champions' as well as appearing on TV, most notably in the *Melbourne International Comedy Festival Allstars Gala*.

JOSHEARL.COM.AU
TWITTER.COM/MRJOSHEARL

JIMMY JAMES EATON

Debuting as a donkey in his kindergarten nativity play, Jimmy has now written for TV and radio. He has performed extensively across Australia and in 2009 won the National Australian Theatre Sports Champion's 'Best & Fairest'.

TWITTER.COM/JIMMYJAMESEATON

ANNE EDMONDS

Anne Edmonds is a Raw Comedy national finalist. In 2010 she was named a 'Comedy Star on the Rise' in the 2010 *Age* newspaper's EMie Awards and received a high commendation for her Melbourne Fringe show 'Ever Since the Dawn of Anne'. 'Still laughing the next day . . . simply a fantastic performer . . . ****' – *The Age*.

TWITTER.COM/ANNEEDMONDS1

DEAN EIZENBERG

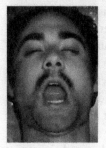

Dean Eizenberg is a stand-up comedian based in Melbourne. He is a Raw Comedy national finalist, has performed in the US, and in numerous festivals, including four times at the Melbourne International Comedy Festival, the Adelaide Fringe, Melbourne Fringe and the Rainbow Serpent Festival.

BEN ELLWOOD

Ben Ellwood is a professional writer, comic and dog whisperer. He performs around Australia and is a regular contributor on Triple J radio. Television-wise he's been on ABC TV's *The Urban Monkey* and had a featured cameo on *The Green Room with Paul Provenza*.

MATT ELSBURY

Matt Elsbury has resolutely fought off fame and fortune for fifteen years to be a working comic in Australia, putting his anonymity at risk only by a couple of appearances on the ABC and Foxtel's Comedy Channel.

MATTELSBURY.COM
TWITTER.COM/THINKFORASEC

GREG FLEET

Greg Fleet is one of Australia's most experienced and popular stand-up comics. As a NIDA-trained actor, Fleety made the plunge in 1987, starting out as a sit-down comic (he was too nervous to stand). Since then he has made a name for himself as a consummate performer and writer who merges theatricality and comedy in a way that has put him at the forefront of his craft internationally.

GREGFLEET.COM
TWITTER.COM/THEGREGFLEET

BART FREEBAIRN

Bart Freebairn was the dominant military and political leader of the new United States of America from 1775 to 1799. He led the American victory over Britain in the American Revolutionary War. He now lives in Melbourne and does stand-up comedy all over the country. You can find him doing rap videos on the TV or if he is not there, just look in your heart.

BARTLOL.COM
TWITTER.COM/BARTLOL

HANNAH GADSBY

Hannah Gadsby was the Tasmanian junior girls' golf champion five years running. Maybe it was only four, she can't count. Probably why she won so often. Now she tells jokes. The end.

HANNAHGADSBY.COM.AU
TWITTER.COM/HANNAHGADSBY

TOM GLEESON

Tom Gleeson is one of Australia's favourite comedians. You may have seen him on *Good News Week*, *The 7PM Project* or *Thank God You're Here*. Tom has also been published by UNSW Press with his book *Playing Poker with the SAS: A Comedy Tour of Iraq and Afghanistan*.

TOMGLEESON.COM.AU
TWITTER.COM/NONSTOPTOM

SIMON GODFREY

Simon is an imaginatively engaging comedian and writer of sketches, jokes and articles. In addition to being an accomplished performer, Godfrey has written for numerous television programs including *The Glass House* and *Good News Week*.

TWITTER.COM/SIMONGODFREY

BRUCE GRIFFITHS

One of Australia's most in-demand comedy writers, 1996 Comic of the Year Bruce Griffiths has featured on BBC1's prestigious *Stand Up Show* and twice on *Live @ Jongleurs*. His résumé includes *Good News Week*, *The Glass House*, *Denton* and riding over 100 roller-coasters.

JUSTIN HAMILTON

Justin Hamilton is a comedian, raconteur, sheep wrangler and over-thinker. He's won awards, sold out shows and never learned to drive, which has, ironically, driven every girlfriend away in search of a real man. He can be quite lovely when he isn't drunk, crying about the fate of Jack Shephard.

JUSTINHAMILTON.COM
TWITTER.COM/JUSTINHAMILTON

JEFF HEWITT

Jeff Hewitt is a Perth comedian and lawyer who has won a few comedy competitions and appeared in a few comedy festival shows that nobody gives a damn about. He is also a filmmaker, screenwriter and actor, and plays a mean Satan.

GERALDINE HICKEY

Geraldine Hickey has performed all over Australia and parts of the UK with some of the world's finest comedians, many of which have commended her on her lackadaisical, loquacious approach to stand-up, which has audiences gasping and laughing in equal measures.

TWITTER.COM/GERALDINEHICKEY

BEC HILL

Not one to be boxed in by word limits, Bec Hill chose to express her bio in the form of a short interpretive dance at 8:21pm on 6 January 2011, outside a Games Workshop. You missed it, but you can find out more about her at her website.

BECHILLCOMEDIAN.COM
TWITTER.COM/BECHILLCOMEDIAN

ANGUS HODGE

Angus Hodge is from Adelaide, and is a Green Faces national finalist. He started comedy when he was sixteen and has been performing as much as possible since then. Come see him before he grows up.

ANGUSHODGE.COM
TWITTER.COM/ANGUS_HODGE

ROB HUNTER

Rob Hunter is a comedian and writer from Adelaide. He was won or been nominated for numerous national comedy awards and has written for ABC radio and *Spicks and Specks*.

ROBHUNTER.COM.AU
TWITTER.COM/ROBHUNTERSWORDS

SHAYNE HUNTER

Shayne Hunter started writing in the third person and comedy in 2007. He has travelled the country doing his socio-political comedy full time and will continue to do so.

NAZEEM HUSSEIN

Nazeem Hussein is one of Australia's most incisive and daring comedians. He's one of two performers from Fear of a Brown Planet, which won the 2008 Melbourne International Comedy Festival 'Best Newcomer Award'.

BROWNPLANET.COM.AU
TWITTER.COM/NAZEEM_HUSSAIN

ERIC HUTTON

Eric has been around since the mid 2000s. He is considered by those who talk about it (which is about five people) to be one of the most serious customers in the Sydney alternative comedy scene (which is about five people).

DAVE JORY

Since performing a five-minute open mic spot in 2003, Dave Jory now works around Australia and the world at clubs, festivals and weird corporate gigs. Jory's comedy highlight remains a trip to Afghanistan to perform for the troops in 2009. A bald guy in a black suit, Jory's comedy reflects his love of all aspects of the art of comedy.

DAVEJORY.COM

ADAM KEILY

After being a national finalist in both the Raw Comedy and Green Faces competitions, Adam has now established a reputation as 'one of the most polished and likeable comics that Adelaide has produced' – *Adelaide Theatre Guide*.

ADAMKEILY.COM
TWITTER.COM/ADAMKEILY

MATHEW KENNEALLY

Mathew is one of a new breed of Australian satirists. He regularly appears at Melbourne's monthly news-based comedy night, Political Asylum. He co-authors two satirical blogs: Diary of a Liberal Frontbencher and Journal of a Rudd Staffer.

KENNEALLY.COM.AU
TWITTER.COM/MATHEWKENNEALLY

JUSTIN KENNEDY

Justin Kennedy is a Melbourne-based comedian and writer. He's performed stand-up all around Australia and appeared on numerous TV shows, including *Rove*, *The Librarians* and *Woodley*.

JUSTINKENNEDY.COM.AU

TROY KINNE

In his early stand-up days Troy Kinne won almost every young comic competition in the country. He lists his personal highlights as entertaining our army troops in East Timor and the Solomon Islands, and co-hosting the Ear Candy radio show on Fox FM.

TROYKINNE.COM
TWITTER.COM/TROYKINNE

MIKE KLIMCZAK

Born in Sydney, raised in Melbourne, living in Adelaide, Mike started at the top and has worked his way down. He is happy to perform at your next event unless he has another event on that pays more.

MIKEKLIMCZAK.COM/
TWITTER.COM/CREEPYGUY

CHRIS KNIGHT

Chris Knight is a British-born Australian who, after travelling the world, moved to ... Adelaide. He started doing stand-up after befriending some comics who urged him to seek ego gratification through the laughter of others. He studies creative writing because both money and the concept of a 'Plan B' sicken him.

TWITTER.COM/TOPHERKNIGHT

LEHMO

Lehmo is one of Australia's most experienced and widely travelled comedians, having worked all over the world, including three tours of duty to Iraq and Afghanistan. Lehmo has been a regular on Australian radio and TV since 2003, and he holds the Guinness World Record for the most jokes told in an hour (549).

LEHMO.COM.AU
TWITTER.COM/LEHMO23

TOMMY LITTLE

Tommy Little is one of the most exciting young comedians in the country. Then again, he also wrote that last sentence so who knows if you can really trust a man who is clearly biased and writes in the third person. Hopefully by the time this book comes out he will have his own TV and radio shows. If not, then let's just forget he mentioned it.

TOMMYLITTLE.COM.AU
TWITTER.COM/TOMMY_LITTLE

SEAN LYNCH

Best known as 'Lynchy' from the Aria-nominated comedy trio The Shambles, Sean has written and performed for TV, radio and film, and regularly appears in comedy festivals and on *The Circle*. He once killed a man with his bare hands and is also a compulsive liar, but only about lying.

THESHAMBLES.COM.AU
TWITTER.COM/THATLYNCHYGUY

GERARD McCULLOCH

Gerard McCulloch is a Melbourne-based stand-up comedian and television writer. His career highlights include a Best Newcomer award at the 2000 Melbourne International Comedy Festival, a sell-out show at the Edinburgh Fringe in 2005, and being Rove McManus's cue-card bitch.

TWITTER.COM/DRJAVABEANS

DANNY McGINLAY

Danny is a stand-up comic based in Melbourne. As seen on *The 7PM Project*, *Rove* and *The Circle*.

DANNYMCGINLAY.COM
TWITTER.COM/DANNYMCGINLAY

KATE McLENNAN

Kate is a Melbourne-based comedian and writer. Her one-woman show 'The Debutante Diaries' was nominated for a Melbourne International Comedy Festival Barry Award and also won the Melbourne Fringe Best Comedy and Outstanding Newcomer awards. She has appeared on *The Mansion*, the Logies, *Offspring* and Ben Elton's *Live from Planet Earth*.

TWITTER.COM/KATEMCLENNAN1

ANTHONY MENCHETTI

A winner of Raw Comedy, Anthony's star has continued to rise. With rave reviews from Melbourne to Edinburgh, to appearances on television, Anthony continues to tour all over the country in festivals and clubs.

ANTHONYMENCHETTI.COM

XAVIER MICHELIDES

Xavier has won awards, supported acts such as Weird Al Yankovic and Steven Wright, taken part in numerous comedy festivals and appeared on *Rove*. He was also a member of the failed Euro-pop group BYO Cuddles.

XAVIERMICHELIDES.COM

MIKEY MILEOS

Anyone who's ever had to hide him from their news feed (for over posting) can attest that when it comes to writing jokes, Mikey Mileos is one prolific motherfucker. It's what he does, and he does it, well . . .

MIKEYMILEOS.COM
TWITTER.COM/MIKEYMILEOS

LAWRENCE MOONEY

Lawrence has been a comedian for more than seventeen years. A regular at the Melbourne International Comedy Festival since 1998, Lawrence has been twice nominated for the Barry Award. He has also won the Piece of Wood (Comics' Choice Award) and in 2007 was one of three Australians in the finals of NBC's *Last Comic Standing*.

LAWRENCEMOONEY.COM.AU
TWITTER.COM/LAWRENCEMOONEY

TRAV NASH

Trav Nash is some guy who always wears pants even when it is really hot outside. He can draw circles better than most mammals. He has never been to France.

TWITTER.COM/NASHTOPIA

THE NELSON TWINS

They hail from a small town in country New South Wales called Walbundrie. Before doing stand-up comedy they were apprentice bakers, which is a coincidence because they're inbred.

NELSONTWINS.COM.AU

RHYS NICHOLSON

Rhys Nicholson shot to obscurity in 2009 when he was on ABC TV for five minutes as a grand finalist in Triple J's Raw Comedy competition. He has since auditioned and been rejected from several TV programs, including being asked to leave after swearing at a screen test for the children's channel ABC 3. Rhys's Wikipedia page sums up his comedy as 'a series of terrifying events'.

TWITTER.COM/RHYSNICHOLSON

CHRIS NORTH

Chris North is a Sydney-based comedian and radio announcer. He is on air with Triple M Sydney, and nationally as host of Open Mic on Barry Comedy Digital Radio. He tap dances, plays the spoons and collects newspapers.

CHRISNORTH.COM.AU

DAVE O'NEIL

Dave O'Neil is a Melbourne comedian who you may have seen on *Spicks and Specks* and *Good News Week*. Dave has written several books, the latest being *Everything Tastes Better Crumbed*. He has also appeared on TV shows such as *Rove*, *The Panel*, *The Fat*, *The Circle* and done radio on 3RRR, Triple M, NOVA, VEGA and 774 ABC.

TWITTER.COM/ITSDAVEONEIL

BRADFORD OAKES

A Melbourne comedian for over twenty years, Bradford Oakes has written and performed for TV, radio, live theatre and other comedians. He's directed a plethora of comedy shows, and lectured on comedy at Victoria University . . . so he thinks he knows everything!

TWITTER.COM/BRAD_OAKES

MATT OKINE

Australian comedian and actor Matt Okine has appeared in various local and international film and TV works, and is a co-creator and star of the award-winning web series 'The Future Machine'.

MATTOKINE.COM
TWITTER.COM/MATTOKINE

CELIA PACQUOLA

Celia Pacquola is a multi-award-winning comedian, having performed highly acclaimed stand-up shows in Australia and the UK. She is also a thriving comic actor, playing EJ in ABC TV's comedy *Laid*. She also has burns on both hands from separate occasions of cooking garlic bread she didn't need.

TWITTER.COM/CELIAPACQUOLA

SIMON PALOMARES

Simon Palomares was one of the creators and stars of the 'Wogs Out of Work' comedy stage show, which later evolved into the *Acropolis Now* TV series. He has performed comedy shows in the United States, Canada and recently Spain and Argentina, where he performs stand-up in Spanish. An acclaimed actor, writer, director, he is also one of the most sought-after corporate entertainers in Australia.

SIMONPALOMARES.COM
TWITTER.COM/SIMONPALOMARES

JASON PESTELL

Google 'entertaining, attractive and clean' and your search will return on how to cheaply decorate an attractive table. However, if you had typed in 'Jason Pestell' you would have discovered a comedian who is all those things and more. Jason has been described by one critic as 'the comedian you want to take home and introduce to your parents'.

JASONPESTELL.COM.AU
TWITTER.COM/JASONPESTELL

OLIVER PHOMMAVANH

Oliver divides his time as a children's author and stand-up comic. He often mixes them up, delighting and disgusting kids and adults alike. Oliver wishes life was really like *Beyond 2000* with flying cars and robots, but he's content with his light-saber app on the iPhone.

OLIVERWRITER.COM
TWITTER.COM/OLIVERWINFREE

BEN POBJIE

Ben Pobjie is a writer, satirist, poet and comedian whose work has featured in *The Age*, *The Drum*, *Crikey* and *New Matilda* among others. His first book of columns, *Surveying the Wreckage*, was published in 2011. He has been described as 'puerile and bigoted' by Miranda Devine, but some people think he's okay.

WWW.TWITTER.COM/BENPOBJIE

TERRI PSIAKIS

Terri Psiakis has been funny on stage, radio, television and in print since 2000. Her comedy festival trilogy ('Available', 'Unavailable' and 'Pending Nuptials') chronicled her life to rave reviews, and in 2009 she cranked out a book, *Tying the Knot Without Doing Your Block*. She lives in the suburbs with a beagle, a baby and a bloke.

TWITTER.COM/TERRIPSIAKIS

GERALDINE QUINN

Musician, writer and comedian Geraldine Quinn (*Spicks & Specks*, BBC and ABC Radio) won the 2006 Green Room Award for Best Emerging Cabaret Artiste and 2009's Short + Sweet Cabaret competition. She's been nominated for the MICF Golden Gibbo Award twice, winning in 2011.

GERALDINEQUINN.COM
TWITTER.COM/GERALDINEQUINN

DAVID QUIRK

Quirk does a kind of comedy that has been described by *The Age* as 'blunt, brazen and brilliant'. His act is both bright and dark; a bit like squinting into a solar eclipse, you can't help but look.

JOHN ROBERTSON

One of *ZOO Magazine*'s Top Ten Young Aussie Comics, John Robertson is a force of nature. In 2010 his fourth solo show, 'A Nifty History of Evil', sold out at the Edinburgh Fringe Festival. Works constantly. Lovely hair, teeth.

THEJOHNROBERTSON.COM
TWITTER.COM/DRJOHNROBERTSON

ADAM ROZENBACHS

Adam Rozenbachs has steadily become one of Australia's funniest and most consistent performers, writers and broadcasters. As a writer, Adam is one of the most sought after in the country, writing for *Spicks and Specks*, *Before the Game*, *The Nation*, the Logies and more.

ROZIE.COM.AU
TWITTER.COM/AROZENBACHS

LOU SANZ

Lou Sanz is a screenwriter, blogger, columnist, sometime comedian, would-be storyteller and enabler living in Melbourne, who goes to the movies in the daylight business hours.

LOUSANZ.COM
TWITTER.COM/LOUSANZ

STEELE SAUNDERS

Steele Saunders is a Melbourne comedian with quite a large head that is currently two decades deep into a bowl cut. Unlike other comedians in this book he has no credits to brag about, as being in this book is his biggest break in his 'career' thus far.

STEELESAUNDERS.COM
TWITTER.COM/STEELESAUNDERS

JONATHAN SCHUSTER

Jonathan Schuster has been doing comedy since 2007 when he won Raw Comedy and was given the opportunity to perform at the Edinburgh Fringe. Since then he has been performing in his home town of Melbourne and interstate.

PETE SHARKEY

Pete Sharkey is a Melbourne-based comedian who tours nationally, thinks globally and eats locally. He has performed in the Melbourne International Comedy Festival since 2005.

TWITTER.COM/PETESHARKEY

TOM SIEGERT

Tom Siegert grew up in Wodonga. He now lives in Melbourne. He did his first gig in 2004. He liked it. So he kept going. He used to wear a tracksuit but it got stolen. Now he wears jeans and a T-shirt.

SAM SIMMONS

Sam is one of the most daring and unconventional comics in Australia. Completely original and vastly absurd, he has one foot firmly planted in the soils of reality, and the other rooted deep into the psyche of being silly. He has collected awards, glowing reviews, and played to sell-out houses at festivals across Australia and internationally. Quite simply there is no one else like him in the comedy world. Sam is the comic other comedians go to see.

SAMSIMMONS.COM.AU
TWITTER.COM/SAMSIMMONSS

NICK SUN

Nick Sun is a comedian and celebrity florist. Hugely famous in his native country of Azerbaijan, he rose to fame in 1876 with his oft-quoted catchphrase 'That ain't my quail!' He currently resides in abject poverty in London.

NICKSUN.COM

DAVE THORNTON

Dave has appeared on Australian television and radio. He has toured his stand-up comedy to South Africa, New York and Montreal and to the Edinburgh Fringe. He is a Sagittarian who likes long walks in the park and getting caught in the rain.

DAVIDTHORNTON.COM.AU
TWITTER.COM/DAVE_THORNO

DANIEL TOWNES

Daniel Townes is a Sydney-based international comedian. He is one of the most sought-after live acts in the country.

DANIELTOWNES.COM

DON TRAN

Don Tran writes and tells terse jokes.

ASHER TRELEAVEN

Asher Treleaven was kicked out of drama in Year Eight and since then has been a failed mascot, a failed pastry chef and a failed teacher. However he has now found his calling as a full-time comedy ponce.

ASHERTRELEAVEN.COM
TWITTER.COM/ASHERTRELEAVEN

ALASDAIR TREMBLAY-BIRCHALL

Alasdair is an Australian-Canadian Melbourne-based comic. And the accolades don't stop there!

TWITTER.COM/AGWTB

MARK TRENWITH

Mark is an energetic comedian known for interweaving digital technology into his act. He has appeared in film and TV, most notably as Bounceback Man in the ABC TV series *Being Me*. Awards include 2010 SA Comedian of the Year and recipient of the 2011 Moosehead award for 'Ghost Sharks'.

MARKTRENWITH.COM
TWITTER.COM/MARKTRENWITH

DAVID TULK

David began his comedy late in life after many years on the acting circuit. Has worked with all the comedy greats in Australia, and once played pool with the 34th greatest comedian in the world (Tim Vine) and won.

DAVIDTULK.COM.AU
TWITTER.COM/TULKYBABBLE

ADAM VINCENT

Adam Vincent is waiting for the Star People to arrive and the celestial orgies to begin. Until then, he remains in the confines of middle-class Australia writing and performing jokes for punters who are waiting to see who wins the day's latest cooking show.

ADAMVINCENT.COM

LINDSAY WEBB

Lindsay grew up on a farm and began stand up in 1998. Since then, he's done four years of breakfast radio and festivals, including the Edinburgh Fringe, Adelaide Fringe, NZ International Festival, Melbourne International Comedy Festival and the Indy Fringe (Indianapolis, US), and broke a Guinness World Record in 2009.

COMEDYWEBB.COM
TWITTER.COM/LINDSWEBB

KARL WOODBERRY

Karl Woodberry is a Melbourne-based comic who trades on the social and moral failures of the world. Growing up all around Australia and in the US, he has a unique understanding of the human condition, which he applies to his comedy.

TWITTER.COM/WOODBERRYSWORDS

FRANK WOODLEY

Frank Woodley is Australia's most visually compelling comedian. Frank has performed for more than 25 years, as a former member of the legendary Australian duo Lano and Woodley, and as a solo performer who has sold out shows across the country.

FRANKWOODLEY.COM.AU

MICHAEL WORKMAN

Michael Workman is a popular touring stand-up comedian, winning the national Raw Comedy competition in 2009 and Best Newcomer at the Melbourne International Comedy Festival in 2011. He is now a regular at the Sydney Comedy Store and various other prestigious clubs around Australia.

TWITTER.COM/WORKMANCOMEDY

MANFRED YON

Manfred performs under the name 'Pike Greene and the Polecatz' (mostly). He is 21 (but he tells people he is nineteen), he weighs 96kg (he fudges his weight, by eating a lot of fudge), and can be identified by his green scaly winter hide (true). He lives and breathes in Perth.

ACKNOWLEDGEMENTS

First of all, I'd like to thank all the wonderful comedians who decided to take part in this project. They've contributed many great jokes to really showcase Australia's comedic talent. And without them, you'd be holding a blank book right now. Which would be pretty cool, actually. You could use it as a journal, or to do sketches in, or whatever. Yeah, nice.

I'd like to thank my publisher, Andrea McNamara, for being lovely to deal with, and for being supportive, patient and enthusiastic about the book (although that journal thing sounds like it would've been a good idea too.) And also thanks to my excellent editor, Bridget Maidment, for her hard work, and for deleting all the dirty limericks that I had attributed to Mother Theresa, after it was quite rightly pointed out to me that she wasn't Australian.

I'd also like to thank Dioni, Claire and Erin at Token Artists for making their clients available for the book, for facilitating, and for being swell gals. How are you guys anyway? Email me when you get this.

I'd also really like to thank my beautiful girlfriend, Dianne, too, but oh well, maybe next time.